FEAR NOT

by
Doren Joseph Gerling

Published by Three Mile Ride LLC

Prole, Iowa, United States of America

ISBN: 979-8-218-90998-7

Printed in the United States of America

Scripture quotations are from the Holy Bible. Scripture quotations may be taken from copyrighted translations. Used by permission or under applicable fair-use provisions. Emphasis added by the author

Dead Poets Honor -- Spoken in truth, kept in faith.

FORWARD

In the 1980s, in my small hometown in Iowa, the Aladdin's Castle arcade in our local mall was *the* place to be for a kid. Parents would sit and visit in the mall's food court with a corndog from the Corndog Factory or maybe a slice of pizza from Guido's. Us kids would rush to the arcade with a handful of quarters. Video games were a new adventure for the mind in those days and little did we know we were also forming lifelong friendships.

This is where I first met Doren, and over the next thirty-five years we have remained friends, traveling through life's adventures, pitfalls, and battles together. I have known him as the kind, skinny kid who was always in the arcade; as the elementary Christian school kid who had to leave an expensive private school and was thrust into public school, where he was bullied and beaten; and as the middle school friend who open-enrolled in my school looking for new friends and a safe place to learn without violence.

He was the friend with whom I spent countless sleepover nights staring at the stars, pondering life's big questions and the possibilities of the future. He became the high school friend and teammate with whom I played baseball, basketball, and football, as we navigated the difficult social dynamics of small-town life together. I have also known Doren as my greatest challenger at board games, where we sharpened our deductive reasoning and strategic planning skills, always knowing that if we weren't the biggest or the meanest, we had better practice being the smartest and most strategic.

Then came the great and challenging college years when we learned that we—and we alone—were responsible for our own successes and failures. We learned to stand back-to-back, protecting not only our dreams, but sometimes our safety as well. Today, I know Doren as the loyal, resolute, warrior-like follower of Christ that he is. His journey was not an easy one and watching him rise and accomplish his dreams alongside my own was one of the greatest joys of my life.

If you are facing troubles, challenging times, or a difficult journey, I believe this book can help you. It is my hope that through Doren's experiences, journeys, and lessons learned, the boulders you carry will become a little lighter—or even be set down altogether—as you discover a deeper faith in God and Jesus. May our Father in heaven grant you strength, understanding, and encouragement on your own adventure, and may you enjoy the journey of this book.

DW

INTRODUCTION

"You'll have bad times, but it'll always wake you up to the good stuff you weren't paying attention to." [*Robin Williams, Good Will Hunting*]

That line has always stuck with me. My favorite actor, Robin Williams, spoke those words through a character who understood pain, trauma, and brokenness. In the movie, he's talking to a young man who has no idea what love looks like, no understanding of what it means to be cared for. He's tough. Hardened. Throw the first punch and ask questions later. Don't take anyone's crap. Emotionally shut off but deeply wounded.

I used to live by movie quotes. No exaggeration, I shaped my thinking around them. And I'll admit, some still hit deep. They carry a kind of wisdom that mixes facts and feelings into something that sounds like truth. But here's the contradiction I came to realize. Facts and truth are not the same. Just because something feels right doesn't mean it's *true*.

Here's another one for you:

"Just because you are a character, doesn't mean you have character."
Go ahead and guess the movie, you can email me about it.

The truth I've found, the kind that transforms, not just informs, comes from our Lord and Savior. His Word isn't just inspirational; it's eternal. I'm not here to knock on movie quotes or the culture they come from, yet they have their place. But we've got to be careful not to treat clever lines as if they're gospel. Don't confuse being "wise" with being right. Don't elevate opinion over the Word of God. Real wisdom comes from God.

You might be wondering what this book is about. Some early drafts had it titled *Relationships.* Then I rewrote, reworked, and renamed it more than once. Why? Because the message evolved as I did. Now, this book is about much more: it is about *fear, weakness, identity, your call from God,* and learning how to move forward with faith.

I've known Christ since the moment I took my first breath. I have trusted Him through childhood, adolescence, and adulthood. I've walked away more times than I would like to admit, but He's always taken me back. Not because I deserved it, but because of His unshakable love and faithfulness. If you hear nothing else from this introduction, hear this: *you are more valuable than you think.* You were designed by God and handcrafted with purpose. Your face, your voice, your body, your heart, all of it was made intentionally by the Creator of the universe. You are His masterpiece.

Not preaching to you. Not trying to impress you. Just talking with you.

I'm not a doctor. I didn't attend seminary. I don't have letters after my name or bestselling books on my shelf. (Yet). But I do have something that matters. *Life experience paired with faith.* I've lived it. I've felt it. I've seen what people go through and I've walked through my own fire.

We all carry something. Trauma. Grief. Anger. Shame. Some of us live in the past; others are stuck in the future. Very few are thinking clearly about the present moment. But the key to growth is learning how to let go of what's behind, live with intention now, and move forward with faith.

I don't have to convince you to listen to me. You do not have to take my advice. You might not change your life tomorrow and that's okay. My goal is to point you to the only source of everlasting change: **God's truth.**

This book is a conversation between us. One that I hope will help you understand yourself better, heal from what's been holding you back and step boldly into who God designed you to be.

Let me be real with you. If someone betrayed you, just let it go. Don't let bitterness take root. It's not worth your peace, your health, or your soul. You don't stop loving someone just because they hurt you. But you *can* forgive them, release them, and move on in freedom. Let God vindicate you. He will. He's just, and He's faithful.

You were not created to live in anger, depression, or despair. You were made for freedom. That doesn't mean you won't cry. That doesn't mean men don't grieve. They feel deeply. They take risks. They're vulnerable. They're kind. Crying doesn't make you weak; it makes you human. But after you've cried, you rise. You step up. You move forward. That's strength. That's masculinity. That's faith.

Living victoriously isn't about perfection. It's about persistence, presence, and power, the kind that only comes from walking daily in faith and courage. This is where our hearts beat in cadence with God's will. This is the chapter of your life where you realize you're not just surviving, you're thriving. Because now, you're not praying for victory, you're praying from victory.

You know you've reached a new place in your walk when you stop begging God for strength and start declaring that you already have it. When you no longer lean on your own understanding but press into His promises. That's why **Deuteronomy 31:6** hits so hard: *"Be strong and courageous. Do not be afraid or terrified because of them, for the Lord your God goes with you; He will never leave you nor forsake you."* It reminds us to be strong and courageous because God goes with us and will never leave nor forsake us.

Victory comes when you start walking in that truth every day. Not just quoting Scripture but living it. Not just believing in God but believing God. It's not theory anymore, it's real. You don't just hear the word; you carry it with you to work, into traffic, into your family arguments, into quiet moments of doubt.

You start realizing that God's Spirit lives inside of you. That the same power that raised Christ from the dead is alive in you. That's not just some "high church language," that's your reality. And when you truly walk in that, the world starts to look different. Fear starts to lose its grip. Anxiety starts to fade. You don't need control because you trust the One who holds everything together.

When you live this way, you're not just a believer, you're a disciple. You're no longer standing on the shoreline of faith; you're in the deep waters with Christ, walking where He walks, following Him wherever He leads.

1 Peter 2:9 calls us a chosen people, a royal priesthood, a holy nation, God's special possession. We were called out of darkness into His marvelous light. And that's the thing; if you're walking daily in faith and courage, then you're walking in the light. Not because you've figured it all out, but because you know the One who has.

Let's get real for a second. Strip away everything; your job, your car, your achievements, your accolades. What do you want most? To be loved. That's the human heart. We all want to be seen, heard, and valued. And we chase that love in people, in accomplishments, in approval. But unconditional love? That only comes from God. People can't give it perfectly. We all fail at it. But God doesn't.

When you truly understand that God loves you; fully, completely, without hesitation, you stop striving for it everywhere else. You stop performing. You start living. And not just living, you live victoriously. Loving others becomes natural when you're rooted in the unconditional love of God. You forgive because you have been forgiven. You serve because He served you first. You speak life because He spoke life into you. That's what it means to walk daily in faith and courage.

And yes, this world is broken. Yes, people will let you down. Yes, pain will still come. But now you know who holds your future. You know what it means to pray from victory. You know what it means to lead, not with ego, but with humility. Not with fear, but with boldness.

And what do you carry with you from this life into the next? Not your bank account. Not your trophies. Just your soul and hopefully the souls of others you've led to Christ. That's what this walk is about. It's people, love, and all about eternity.

So, we walk daily. We walk courageously. We walk in love. We walk with purpose. We walk like Jesus did. And when we fall, which we will, we get back up. We don't wallow.

We don't quit. We remember that Jesus prayed from victory on the cross, even when it looked like defeat. And three days later, He proved that nothing could stop God's plan. Now it's our turn. To walk daily. To walk in power. To live loved. And to live victoriously. And here's the truth: you don't have to be perfect to live victoriously. You **must** be committed. You must be honest about who you are, about your flaws, about your failures and still choose to walk forward. Still choose faith. Still choose love. That's what the daily walk with Christ looks like. It's messy. It's humbling. But it's powerful.

And it's not about how you feel every day. There are going to be days you don't feel strong. You might not even feel saved. But you are. Because salvation isn't a feeling, it's a fact sealed by the blood of Jesus. And courage? It doesn't mean you're never afraid. It's believing without seeing. He won't leave when you're doubting, or you're overwhelmed. Not even when you've messed it all up again. He's staying. And He's still calling you chosen.

This is what means to live victoriously knowing the enemy can't have you. That your past doesn't define you. That no matter what pit you've fallen into, God's hand is already reaching down to pull you back up. It's about living like the fight's already been won, because it has. When you wake up in the morning, the enemy should be nervous. Because you're choosing faith over fear. Because you're walking in truth, not trauma. Because you've started to understand that your strength comes from a source that doesn't run dry.

"I can do all things through Christ who strengthens me." - **Philippians 4:13**

Not some things. All things.

And when you walk in that identity, when you walk in that boldness and humility at the same time, you are dangerous, in a good way. You're lighting up dark places. You're breaking generational curses. You're speaking life over your kids, your coworkers, your community. You're not perfect, but you're powerful because you've surrendered.

This is what the victorious life looks like: it's rooted in Scripture, grounded in prayer, filled with love, and lived out through daily obedience. It's real. It's raw. But it's holy. Because when Jesus is at the center of it, even your mess becomes ministry.

Living victoriously isn't about arriving at some spiritual height where life is easy and polished. It's about showing up every day, broken sometimes, worn out, unsure, but still choosing to walk in faith and courage because you know who walks with you. It's about surrender. It's about obedience. It's about love. It's about trusting that even when you feel empty, God is still pouring. Even when you feel weak, God is still strong. Even when you feel like you're just holding on by a thread, He's already holding you.

Victory isn't a destination. It's a posture. It's a mindset. It's a daily decision. When you live like that, when you wake up and say, "Lord, use me today," when you keep loving people even when they don't love you back. When you keep forgiving even when it hurts, you're not just surviving anymore. You're thriving. You're living in victory. You're walking out the very purpose God designed for you even before you were born. Because that's what chosen people do. That's what royal priests do. That's what sons and daughters of the King do.

So, live like it. Speak like it. Pray like it. Love like it. You were made for this. You were made to walk in faith. You were made to walk in courage. And by the Spirit of God inside you, you were made to live victoriously.

Forever and always, from victory, not for it. Amen.

"Open my eyes to see the wonderful truths in your instructions." - **Psalms 119:18**

This is one of my favorite verses in the entire Bible. It's not just words, it's a request, a posture of surrender. A desire to see *clearly* what God is trying to teach us, even when life clouds our vision.

This may end up being a book about fears and relationships, but really, it's always been about something deeper: God's truth. His love, and how we keep moving forward; through joy, heartbreak, healing, and everything in between. He's walked with me through childhood and into adulthood. I've rebelled. I've wandered. And every time I've come back, He's been right there waiting. He is sovereign, faithful, and full of love that doesn't flinch when we mess up.

Here's something you might need to hear right away.

You are more special than you can even understand. You are loved, designed by God, completely.
Everything about you.
Your face. Your laugh. Your personality, Your quirks. Your strength. Your sensitivity. You are His creation, His masterpiece, His child.

So where am I going with all of this?

We're heading on a journey. A deep dive into the heart of what God says about who we are, how we relate to each other, and how we can stay grounded in truth while navigating a world that often seems upside-down.

Now I'll introduce myself.

I'm a former police officer from the beautiful state of Iowa. My job used to be about facts, what happened, when, where, and who did it. If you ran a red light, the video told the truth. If you got into a car accident, I pieced together the details to figure out who was at fault. And in the darker corners of the job, I looked for signs, evidence, and wounds. Truth wasn't a matter of opinion. It was my job to uncover it.

But even before and long after I clocked out of that role, I lived through my own share of trauma, healing, and growth. I've worked in the restaurant industry and law enforcement. This is me saying: I've seen some stuff. I've felt some things. I've seen enough to understand fear. I've stared down the brokenness in others and in myself. My call has been the protector for those who just need someone to sit with in their pain. Just for a moment and not flinch at their story. To walk with them in empathy.

Strip it all away, the money, the jobs, the accolades, the trauma, the failure, the masks. What we're really chasing is unconditional love. I've come out of all of it with hard truth. Most of us are chasing it in people who were never created to give it back. So, we end up broken, bitter, and confused when they don't deliver.

But God can. And God does.
Even when we don't see it. Even when we don't feel it.

Even when life hands us betrayal instead of loyalty, silence instead of answers.

That's what this book is about.
It's a love letter from a flawed, healing man who's walked through fire and wants you to know you're not alone. We were built to love and be loved.

It's about faith, forgiveness, moving forward, and the kind of courage it takes to still believe in love when it's wounded you. And listen, I'm not a psychologist. I don't have a PhD in relationships or some fancy couch I sit behind while you're pouring out your heart. What I *do* have is life experience. I've had to forgive people who didn't ask. I've loved people who walked away. I've been hurt by people I trusted. And through it all, I've chosen to grow closer to God. I ran to him, not from Him.

If you've ever been betrayed by someone you loved. If you've ever struggled to figure out who you are anymore. If you're tired of pretending you're okay when your heart is shattered.
Then this is for you.

And hear me on this. Being **real** doesn't mean you're stone-cold, arrogant, or stoic all the time. It means you feel, you live, and you keep going anyway. It means you cry, but you don't drown. It means you face your pain, and then you give it to God.

This book is messy. It jumps around sometimes. Just like real life. Just like real healing.

I'm not here to tell you what to do.
I'm here to walk with you as you figure it out.
I'm here to tell you God still loves you. You're still worthy.

And your best days. They're not behind you. They're ahead.

So, welcome to the journey.
We're not going backwards.
We're taking the step *forward*. In cadence with faith, courage, and with our eyes wide open to the truth.

FEAR NOT.

FEAR AT YOUR GATE

"Do not be afraid or discouraged, for the Lord will personally go ahead of you. He will be with you; He will neither fail you nor abandon you." - **Deuteronomy 31:8**

Who Do you fear? Is it the true you?

Every day I make choices about what clothes I wear to the gym, which water bottle I grab on the way out the door. And yeah, sometimes I choose the stained shirt. Sometimes I choose a bad attitude. Sometimes I even choose gossip, because it feels good going down but burns in the pit of my stomach later. It ruins relationships. And I know better.

But that's not who I want to be. I want to be better in character. I want to be stronger in spirit.

So why do we fear? Because we don't know what's going to happen. We play out scenarios in our minds like a movie reel, faster than real life can even catch up. Fear rises out of that uncertainty. It exposes our insecurities and hands us every excuse we need to freeze in place. Fear exposes our insecurities and validates the excuses we use to stay stuck. It freezes us.

But when we walk with God, when we choose faith over fear, something shifts. We stand up. We are pushing forward. We take risks. We show vulnerability. And we trust that He is going before us, just like He promised. The enemy stands at the gate, making you believe you don't have the key. He'll whisper that you're not ready, not worthy, not enough. But God is on the other side of that door—waiting with purpose, with calling, with destiny. You must ask yourself: what's stopping me? Embarrassment? The fear of looking foolish? The lies others have spoken over you.

We say we want to grow, but we resist failure. Yet growth and failure are inseparable.

So, stop waiting for validation. If destiny is on the other side of that door, give it your all. Ask God for the key. And if He wants you to search for it, then ask Him where to begin.

Lord, show me where to start looking. Show me how to think, how to believe, how to trust.

The truth is: we cannot do this alone. If we keep trying to fight in our own strength, we'll keep failing. The reason fear keeps winning is because we're trying to win the battle with flesh when it was always meant to be fought in the spirit. Satan wants us to get tired so he can devour us.

Somehow, we put aside the obvious danger that Satan is ferociously powerful. However, it's all smoke. He thinks he's going to win. We outnumber Satan and all his lemmings we are pitted against. But here's the truth: Satan only fights so hard because he knows he's already defeated. Evil is just hanging on, clawing, refusing to accept loss, and refusing to grow. Lies and trickery is what defines Satan's role. He wants to rebuke growth and transformation. He does not want us or you to become anything else. If he stopped selling lies, he'd no longer exist. Lies can only ever remain lies. Trickery can only ever remain trickery. Satan will always be Satan. Lies stop. Death stops. Growth is continuous and never stops. Death to the flesh, life in the Spirit.

The problem? Most of us never make it through. We're scared. We've never stood long enough to face the opposition. We've never stayed planted when it got uncomfortable. So, we run. We hide. We fear the embarrassment of falling flat on our face.

But failure is part of growth. You cannot grow unless you're willing to trip, to get scraped up, to look a little foolish on the way. So why do we care so much about what other people think? Why do we let their opinions keep us from walking through that door?

But with God, we stand tall. With God, we fight. In faith. In confidence. In vulnerability. In bold, risk-taking obedience.

Fear stands at the gate to our destiny. That gate may look locked. It may look like there's no way through. But sometimes, what we think is a gate is just a door, and on the other side of that door is everything God's been preparing for us.

If your destiny is what you desire, why not give everything you've got to go after it?

Ask God for the key. And if He doesn't hand it over right away, ask Him where to start looking. Ask for wisdom, for direction, for insight. Because you will not get there alone.

The reason we keep failing is because we keep trying to do it without Him.

Fear is just a feeling. It's rooted in anticipation of something that hasn't even happened yet. So why are you afraid?

You're letting something that doesn't even exist keep you from the life that could be. That's not what God has for you.

He wants you to walk boldly into your calling. But that means you're going to have to face the fear head-on. That fear? It's the final barrier between where you are and where you're called to be. God isn't going to remove it until you've grown strong enough to stand in front of it and say, "Move."

This is growth. This is the test. You've got to stand in the storm. You've got to face the fire and still trust God with the outcome.

No one can take from you what's meant for you. God has already gone ahead. He's already in your future, working out the details. You don't have to chase what's yours; you must be obedient and faithful enough to show up and go through the door.

Bring God into the storm. Into the fire. Into your doubt.

Be responsible. Be accountable. Be patient. Be disciplined. All these things are required on the Christian Walk. You cannot fake your way through this.

Obey the greatest commandments:
Love the Lord your God.
Love your neighbor as yourself.

It's not complicated, but it is difficult.

I'm an encourager. I'm someone who seeks action through inspiration and discipline. I've got cadence, paired with charisma. I don't just want to motivate you, I want to help you shift your mindset and change how you think, how you move, how you walk.

Stop letting other people's opinions dictate your pace. Yes, I know you're listening to me right now, but all I'm doing is repeating what God already said. He is the one you need to hear from. I'm just a voice pointing you back to Him.

I can't fix you. But He can.

He placed me here to help guide people into becoming spiritual leaders in their homes, in their communities, in their calling. You might feel like a dead tree right now, but through Christ, that tree can bloom again.

God wants to open your eyes to see what He sees in you. He wants to give you vision, clarity, and purpose. But you've got to move first.

This is your part. Be the light in the darkness. Stay vigilant. Be dependable. Love everyone. Spread the Word.

"Whatever you do, do it from the heart, like you're doing it for the Lord, not for people." - **Colossians 3:23**

So, I pray: Lord, keep my mind clear and my spirit open. Let me hear Your voice. Teach me discipline. Grow me. Help me be patient. Help me lead with love.

This is about motivation. Discipline. Growth. Leadership. Risk. Faith. Vulnerability. Courage. I've worked on myself over the years and I'm still working towards the man God wants me to become. But I'm not afraid anymore, because I'm at peace. No matter what life throws at me, I know God is already ahead of me, making a way.

Fear God, not man. Live with reverence and walk in wisdom. When sin knocks, let your attitude and actions reflect the armor you wear.

Put on the full armor of God: - *Ephesians 6:14*

- **The Belt of Truth**

- **The Breastplate of Righteousness**

- **The Shoes of Peace**

- **The Shield of Faith**

- **The Helmet of Salvation**

- **The Sword of the Spirit**

God has your back. Jesus leads your path. The Holy Spirit lives in you.

You never have to retreat. And I choose to walk in that truth.

FAITH IS YOUR ANTIDOTE

Overcoming fear through faith. What a powerful truth that is. If you ask me, it's incredible how faith can become our antidote to fear. We've talked about the different things that fear brings on; anxiety, apprehension, even aggressive reactions stemming from our natural fight-or-flight instincts. These aren't just emotional responses; they're psychological shifts in our behavior.

So, here's the core of it: when we talk about faith being an antidote, we're talking about making God your number one. When fear rises, you don't have to be afraid anymore. You slow it down. Anxiety speeds things up; it overstimulates your mind and overwhelms you. This flood of "what-ifs" and worst-case scenarios is exactly what Satan wants. It's all about getting you to imagine the worst. To stir up discouragement and despair and trap you in your own thoughts.

But what if you slowed it all down? What if you stopped letting your imagination become your enemy? Evil wants you to overreact, to become emotionally hijacked by the moment, so you'll let it define your future. You begin telling the story of what happened over and over again until it lives with you, but here's the thing: the event is already in the past. It only has power if you keep dragging it into your future. Faith disrupts that pattern. The earlier you reach for faith, the better. It's like taking an antidote before the poison spreads. You want to prevent fear from penetrating your soul, from sinking into your spirit. Once fear gets deep enough, it begins to affect your identity, your direction, your purpose. That's where trauma, hopelessness, and bitterness start to grow.

And remember, nowhere in the Bible does it promise that following Christ will make your life easy. In fact, it promises quite the opposite. You will have trials. But when you take up your cross and follow Him, it's worth every battle and every hardship. Because God is more powerful than anything you're facing. Faith is more powerful than your circumstances.

Maybe you're facing financial pressure, or you've been rejected by a school or had a relationship fall apart. Maybe you're dealing with a tough diagnosis. These moments are real, but faith gives us a way through them. We often fear that our situation has the power to define who we are or determine what's next. But it doesn't. Faith does.

I know this personally. I've had relationships fall apart. I've had moments I thought would destroy my future. But I'm still here. I'm talking to you now. And what got me through was faith. I refused to let fear convince me that my future was over.

You might feel like giving up because one important thing didn't work out. But maybe that one thing wasn't your everything. Maybe you put all your hope into that one person, your career, or a dream home. But God has more. He's still right beside you. Faith reminds you that your identity is not wrapped up in your circumstances, but in your Creator.

So how do you cultivate that kind of faith, especially in moments of doubt and uncertainty? For starters, it's deeply personal. I can only tell you what has worked for me, but I promise you, there is a way. It's up to you to **want** that relationship with God and seek the answer in Him.

Christianity isn't a hidden trick or secret society. It's simple but profound: you must believe without seeing. That's the essence of faith. We live in a world where seeing is believing, but that can be deceptive. There's an old saying: "Believe none of what you hear and only half of what you see." And in today's world, video media can be easily manipulated. So, seeing isn't always believing. The truth is that the most powerful beliefs often come from the ones you can't see.

So how do you build that kind of belief? Through prayer. I talk to God all day long. And yes, I really mean all day. God isn't some distant figure; He's with you every moment. He's not bound by flesh like we are. He is Spirit. He is the great **I AM**. And He loves you deeply. He wants you to come to Him with your problems.

When you pray, you're not just speaking into the air. You're releasing your burdens to someone who already knows them. But more than that, you're inviting Him to act on your behalf. And yes, sometimes you don't hear an answer right away, but that does not mean He's not working. Often, He's already made a way.

Let go of the need to control everything. Some parts of life are simply too heavy for human strength. And that's okay. Rely on God. Drop off your burdens in prayer and then leave them there. Don't keep dragging them around. That's where fear and anxiety creep back in. Your job is to maintain self-control and spiritual discipline. This walk with Christ is not easy. It's not supposed to be. But it is worth it. There is love, peace, strength, wisdom, comfort, and growth along this path. You'll be challenged, but you'll also be changed.

At the end of the day when it's quiet again, pray. And when you pray, thank Him. If you've already asked Him for something, you don't need to keep begging. Just thank Him that it's on the way. Praise Him for hearing you. Don't go back complaining, "Why hasn't it happened yet?" Because sometimes He's growing you first. Sometimes He's preparing you to carry the blessing you asked for.

When God says, "Be still," then, be still. And when He says, "Go," you go. Don't miss your opportunities. Pay attention. Every single day matters. Even the quiet uneventful ones. Stop treating any day like it's ordinary. Every day, God is speaking. Every day, He's sending signs, people, moments of insight. You must pay attention.

Start your morning expecting to hear from Him. Go through your day listening. Watch who He puts in your path. Pray throughout the day. Spend time just sitting with Him. Yes, He already knows your heart, but He still wants you to talk to Him. That relationship is where your strength is built.

And when it comes to building faith, the Bible is essential. Read it. Even if it's difficult at first, stick with it. God's

Word is alive. It speaks into every season of life. Sure, there are great podcasts and helpful books, but they're not the source, only tools. The Bible is your source, and it contains only the truth.

And if you're struggling to stay in the Word, get into community. Join a men's or women's group. Find a mentor. Surround yourself with people who are further along in the journey, people who can guide you, challenge you, and walk with you. Ideally, you should have mentors for different areas of life, faith, finances, family, career.

You don't have to walk this out alone. Faith isn't just cultivated in private; it grows in community too. And when you combine prayer, scripture, and spiritual mentorship, you'll begin to see your faith become stronger than your fears.

God's got you. Even when you don't see the way forward, He does. Trust Him. Walk with Him. And remember faith is the antidote to fear.

WALKING FORWARD

How am I supposed to write this book? That's what I used to ask myself. How do I stay focused when distractions surround me? How do I leave a sermon fired up and end up slipping right back into my old habits?

Here's the answer: **God is still with you.**

His Spirit is in you. His Word still stands. He's already made a way.

So, take that step. Walk toward your fear. Don't let the enemy crush your dreams. Don't let people project their limits onto your destiny.

"For this reason, I suffer as I do. But I am not ashamed, for I know whom I have believed." -**2 Timothy 1:12**

Fear is the anticipation of what hasn't even happened yet. It's the "what ifs" that paralyze us. It's the illusion of danger that hasn't even arrived. But God says *don't be afraid,* because He's already there. Instead of the typical "what if it doesn't," project confidently in Faith and speak out, what if it does?

Let God work for you, not just around you. Bring Him into your storm. Into your confusion. Into your waiting. This requires discipline. It requires patience. It requires love. Life requires faith.

You must learn how to walk in cadence with Christ, step for step, even when the way isn't clear.

I don't claim to be perfect. Even on a good day, I'm still learning how to apply this in my own life. Just today, I was short with my mom. She said something I didn't like, and I snapped. I was frustrated. I didn't show patience or self-control, and that's not okay. But I recognize it, and I'm choosing to grow through it.

This is what real repentance looks like: recognizing your sin, confessing it, receiving God's mercy, and walking in grace. I prayed right after. "Lord, I was snappy with my mom. I let my emotions get in the way. Please forgive me. I seek Your mercy, and I receive Your grace." Additionally, apologize to them for your emotional reaction. I promise you, they will understand.

We all have those moments where our tongue speaks before our spirit can catch it. Where our brokenness wins the argument. But when you are walking with God, you don't have to stay in that place. You're not condemned. You're corrected, but you're also loved, restored and reminded of who you are in Him.

Don't let guilt linger. Don't let the enemy tell you you're too far gone. That's a lie. The devil wants to trap you in shame, but God invites you into freedom.

Yes, your heart is wicked. But your soul is saved.

The things you do wrong are already forgiven. You don't have to be perfect. But you do have to be real. Be honest with God. Love Him back the way you love people who don't even have the power to save you.

God is the constant. People will hurt you. Disappoint you. Leave you. But His love will never fail.

Love is patient. Love is kind. It doesn't boast. It isn't proud. Love does not dishonor. It doesn't keep a record of wrongs. Love always protects. Always hopes. Always perseveres.

Love. Is. Everything.

And if you want to grow, if you want to overcome fear, you must receive that love. Then you live it. Speak it. Share it. Walk it out. Some days I wake up and feel the enemy knocking at my door. Whispering that I'm not good enough. That I've messed up too many times. That I'll never get where I'm trying to go. That's when I dig deep. I remind myself of who I am in Christ.

I am loyal. I am committed. I am truthful. I put my all into what I do. I have a good heart. I see the good in others, even when they can't see it in themselves. I'm strong. I'm courageous. I'm vulnerable. I take risks because of my faith. I'm an encourager. I lead with discipline and inspiration. I speak God's truth, not mine. I'm here because God placed me here to help others walk in endurance, in courage, and in Spirit-led faith.

So, trust Him. Even when you don't understand what He's doing. Even when it's uncomfortable. Even when you're standing in uncertainty. Remember Lot's wife. Don't look back. Fear will try to drag you back into old patterns. It will use your past to convince you you're not ready for your future. But God is already ahead of you.

Fear is the enemy's favorite tool. It's anticipation of danger. It's anxiety over what might be. It's the urge to freeze when God is telling you to move. Fear is not from God. The only fear you should carry is a *holy* fear, a deep awe and reverence for who He is. Not for fear of punishment, but honor for His power, love, and authority in your life.

"The Lord is for me, so I will have no fear. What can mere people do to me?" - **Psalm 118:6**

You don't need to be afraid of what people say. You don't need to fear failure. You don't need to doubt what God has already spoken over your life.

So let go of the fear. Embrace the unknown. Ask the questions:
What do I need to grow?
What do I need to change?

Start with yourself. Start with His Word. And remember:

"So don't worry about tomorrow, for tomorrow will bring its own worries. Today's trouble is enough for today." - **Matthew 6:34**

Let God refine you. Let Him shape you. Let Him lead.

We're just getting started.

FAITH IN MOTION

Fear is a constant visitor in our lives. It often shows up before we even take action; spinning scenarios in our minds, replaying stories we've heard or experienced, making us question ourselves before we start. But faith invites us to step beyond those mental chains and walk boldly forward, trusting God to guide us through.

One of the most powerful tools to overcome fear is prayer. Prayer is more than just words spoken—it's an open invitation for God to be part of your daily life. Whether you have family, friends, or loved ones around you, it's God who gives the wisdom, strength, and guidance you need. You might have parents, siblings, a spouse, or even in-laws who support you. That's a blessing, but none of those relationships replace the personal connection you build through prayer. God cares about every detail of your life, from your smallest worries to your biggest dreams.

When you pray, you invite God to walk with you through your fears and challenges. The Holy Spirit inside you speaks truth and love, always pointing you back to God's promises in Scripture. This is your foundation, your anchor, when the waves of fear try to pull you under.

Alongside prayer, scripture is your daily guidebook. Every answer, every word of comfort, every encouragement you seek is waiting for you in God's Word. Meditation on these truths helps quiet the noise of fear. Worship is another powerful tool, lifting your heart in praise not only shifts your focus away from fear but fills you with peace and strength to face the day.

But faith is not just about quiet reflection. It calls you to action. When God nudges you to move forward, take that step, even if your fear is loud. Whether it's applying for a job, starting a new project, or pursuing a dream. Action produces faith as the antidote to fear. I remember applying for my dream job multiple times and hearing "no" over and over. The waiting, the tests, and the comparisons to others were tough. Fear whispered, "You're not good enough." But every time I showed up and tried, I learned something. Every attempt brought growth. If I had quit before trying, that would have been the real failure.

Your fears may be rooted in past experiences, stories you've heard, or even the influence of social media and the world's noise. But God's truth stands above all of it. Fear is a tactic of the enemy, designed to keep you stuck. The Holy Spirit, however, leads you into truth and empowers you to move past what holds you back.

Remember this: your fears are often more in your mind than reality. When you finally step onto that field, into that test room, or toward that new opportunity, fear loses its power. Action dissolves it. You prove to yourself that you are stronger than your doubts.

There will be days when the journey feels overwhelming. When you don't know if you're enough or if you're doing the right thing. That's when you turn again to prayer, Scripture, meditation, and worship. Let these be the tools you carry with you every day.

Be grateful for where you are, even if it's not where you want to be yet. Praise God for the steps you're taking, the desires He's placed in your heart, and the patience you're cultivating as you wait on His perfect timing. Faith is trusting that God's plan is better than our own, and that every step you take in obedience is moving you closer to your destiny.

God loves you deeply. He is with you in every struggle, every fear, and every victory. When you combine prayer, scripture, meditation, worship, and action, you are building a life that fear cannot shake. Take that step today. Trust Him and watch how He turns your fear into your greatest testimony.

BOUNDARIES OF THE HEART

I'll be the first to admit, I still struggle with setting boundaries, especially with the people I let get closer.

Now don't get me wrong, I'm not saying I let people walk all over me. But this is something different. It's not just about physical space; it's about emotional and spiritual parameters. It's something deeper. I'm still building my character. Still becoming. And I know that what we say to people flows from what's inside of us. That's why I don't want my speech to happen too quickly. I want to process. I want to think. I want to be slow to speak so I don't make emotional decisions in the heat of the moment.

My dear brothers and sisters, understand this: Everyone should be quick to listen, slow to speak, and slow to anger, for human anger does not accomplish God's righteousness.
- James 1:19-20

This is where the inside spills out.

The anger. The rage. That pent-up fire that's been hiding in you for years, not even because of the person standing in front of you right now, but because they're pressing buttons someone else installed a long time ago.

And when they press your buttons, we go off. But we're not really going off on *them*, are we? We're reacting to the memory of someone else. An old wound. A familiar pain. Some of us, on the other hand, don't lash out. We keep it quiet. Real quiet. We bottle it up. Seal it and smile through it. And then? We go about our day, replaying that loop in our heads. Over and over again. By the afternoon, we've run twenty different scenarios of what we *should've* said. What we *could've* done. But we didn't. And now we're mad. Not at anyone else, but at ourselves.

So, the next person that crosses that same invisible line? They get all of it. The explosion. The fire. The wrath that was never meant for them. They're catching heat from the last one, and the one before that, and the one before that. See, here's the catch—some of us carry that anger for *days*. It sits in us like a slow-burning fire. We start talking about it. We gossip. We call people just to talk about what *they* did to *us*. But what does that really do? You're not talking to *them*. You're not seeking resolutions, you're seeking validation. But why? Why not talk to God? Why not go to the person and speak the truth? Why are we holding on to something that's eating us alive?

Maybe it's because we're waiting. Waiting to gather ammunition from everyone we talk to, so we can go back and unleash all our hurt, dressed up in other people's opinions. But here's the thing: that darkness you're about to release? It didn't come from *them*. It came from a moment long ago. A trigger. A trauma you never dealt with.

And now? You're dragging those unhealed wounds into new situations with people who don't even know your story. They didn't know it hurt. They didn't know they were stepping on landmines. But that's how it starts. You begin to destroy yourself from the inside out with this kind of thinking. It corrodes your character. It bruises your faith. It poisons your joy. You can't live like that. You can't keep holding on to these offenses. Let them out. But do it with wisdom. Ask God for advice, but don't gossip. Talk about *you*. What can *you* do to not feel this way toward them? Can you ask Him to show you the mirror to your heart?

Look deep inside. Ask Him the hard questions: Why do I feel this way? Why do I act like this?
Why do I snap when people press buttons they don't even know exist? Pray. Ask the Holy Spirit to help you capture those thoughts. You are responsible for your peace. You are responsible for your reactions. Patience. Because sometimes, people really are just evil. Let's be honest. Some folks are just looking to provoke you. They know how you'll react. Your reaction is their fuel. Their ego. But don't give it to them. Write it out. Journal it. Get it all out before you bring it to them. Then, when you're ready—send the letter. Or better yet, sit down and have a face-to-face conversation.

Let God handle it. Let Him deal with the revenge. You don't have to play that game. There's no shame in walking away. No embarrassment in silence. No weakness in self-control. Yes, sometimes you may need to speak up and reestablish boundaries but let God lead first. Because most of the time, they hurt too. That's why they act like that. That's why they push. The great part is this: when you walk through this the right way, God's way, you're not only protecting yourself, but you also get to help someone else. And you might just see healing on both sides.

God has a reason for all of it. He's trying to bring us back to intimacy with Him. But if we walk around with wrong ideas in our head, we'll make it harder to hear His voice. He takes the initiative. He leads the dance. All we must do is obey and step into the relationship. *Jeremiah 10:10* says He is the true and living God. He's not out here to play games with our emotions. He speaks truth. Don't test God. Don't put Him on trial. Miracles aren't toys; they're reminders that nature bows to the One who made it. True faith? That's trusting without seeing.

The Bible is full of divine guidance. It's not superstition, it's sacred. If you want answers, start there. Don't go chasing signs in the sky, seek His voice in the Word. In prayer. He will confirm what's from Him. God doesn't lie. His promises always come to pass. And if it's truly from Him, there will be confirmation, real, tangible evidence. Not confusion. Never chaos. Because He's not the Author of confusion. So, if you're confused, pause. He'll give you wisdom if you ask. He will make the path clear.

Every decision is either a step toward God or a step away. There are always causes and effects. The Bible teaches us that. Proverbs tells us that hard work brings reward. But not just any work, *wise* work. *Intentional* work. So, pray. Ask God for clarity. He gives it to those who seek Him with an open heart. Don't force meaning onto things. You'll know when it's from Him. And if you're still in doubt? Ask Him again.

He'll make it known. Always.

WALKING IN HIS CADENCE

I'm here to speak. To talk about some of the things I've been walking through lately. Something inside my spirit has shifted. I don't even know the right word to describe it. Is it solidarity? Is it a deeper connection? I can't always find the vocabulary. But the moment I open my mouth, the words come. The moment I start speaking into this microphone, the metaphors rise up, the parallels between life and the Word of God start forming in my mind, and suddenly—it all makes sense.

God tells us to pay attention. Not just to the big things. To the small, every day, moment-by-moment things. He asks us to live each day. Really live it. That doesn't mean being careless. It doesn't mean quitting your job out of anger or walking away from something just because it feels uncomfortable. It means to be present. Be mindful. Don't let your pain spill out and hurt other people. And don't let your success turn into pride that pushes people away.

Some people won't understand you. Let them go. They'll set their own table, and that table will become their own trap. You don't have to fight it. You don't have to chase clarity from people who aren't willing to grow. Let them be. Let God deal with them.

When you wake up—whether it's 4:00 AM for the gym or your kids crawling on you or your alarm for work—pay attention. Because God is already speaking to you. Every time you sweat for a dream, every time you cry out in pain, every time your heart breaks over something you've been praying for—He sees it all. He sees the tears, the sleepless nights, the whispered prayers, the frustration, the disappointment, the loneliness. And yes, even the joy you imagined you'll feel when those prayers are answered!

You put in work. You bled for some of this stuff. And still, nothing seems to happen. You keep pushing, and it feels like you're standing still. But that's faith. That's growth. That's what it looks like. Slow. Frustrating. But real.

We are talking about fear, weakness, and learning how to recognize the enemy's voice and silence it with truth. Because most of the time, the enemy isn't yelling. He's whispering. Whispering doubts. Whispering insecurities. Whispering lies that sound like your own voice.

You hear it when someone judges you. When they talk down to you about your job, your car, your savings, or your clothes. When someone changes their mind about you after telling you they loved you. When someone walks away because fear got in the way of their faith. And even though you know God brought them into your life, you still end up the one hurt. And now you're left trying to forgive. Trying to let go. Trying to believe that God will bring something better.

He saw the vision you imagined. The life you pictured.

Of course, there are wonderful truths you don't even know about yet. Things you can't see are already happening on your behalf. Answers are formed into questions you haven't even learned to ask. Right now, in your storm, in your silence, God is moving.

Yes, you can get advice from other people. And there's nothing wrong with that. But the deepest truth you need will always come from God Himself. Turn to Him when the storm rages and the furnace burns. When everything in you wants to give up, *don't.* Surrender it all to Him instead.

It's like trying to stop yourself from singing when your favorite worship song hits during church. You don't hold back; you lift your voice. That's what surrender feels like.

Foundation*: The support upon which everything rests.* According to Merriam-Webster, that's the definition. Your foundation is Christ. He offers you faith through salvation. Through the sacrifice of His Son, your sins are covered. But repentance is a daily walk. It's not about being perfect, it's about being honest. Every day, look in the mirror and ask yourself who you really are, what you believe, and whether your actions match your faith.

We have free will. We have self-control. And we have the ability to be real with ourselves and others. I've got my flaws. I've got my silly sins and slip-ups. And so do you. That's the beauty of the gospel; *we are not perfect, but we are being perfected.*

Paul talks about this in Romans. We want to live by the Spirit. It's not easy, but it's possible. We fight thoughts that aren't true. We assume the worst. We let betrayal or pain bury our joy. But none of that is your identity. God brings you back every time.

If you're struggling, talk to someone. Find someone who sees the real you and can hold you accountable. Don't hold bitterness inside. It festers into resentment and weighs down your spirit. Sometimes it's not even about what someone did, it's what life did to you. Either way, you don't have to carry it alone.

That's why I'm here. He sent me. That's why this book exists. I'm here to encourage you, to help you walk toward self-sufficiency in faith, and to remind you that you are not alone. We learn from each other. Even if you're in the middle of a storm, you have something to teach me. That's mutual mentorship. That's humility. That's how God works. Truth comes from God's Word. My experience is real, but yours is too. We may not have lived the exact same stories, but if you and I sat down, you'd look at me and ask, "You get it?" Yes, I do.

Let me nudge you, move *you* into action. You've been dreaming about change, but dreams don't move without action. The enemy will use distractions to keep you stuck. So, let's confront that. We face a spiritual enemy every single day. People may betray, hurt, or even attempt to destroy your character. Some are filled with jealousy and envy, and they see you as a threat. Keep those people at a distance. Love them, but don't give them access to your spirit.

Do what is right the first time.

"Trust in the Lord with all your heart, and do not rely on your own understanding; in all your ways know him, and he will make your paths straight." - **Proverbs 3:5-6**

Trust in the Lord with all your heart. Don't lean on your own understanding. Not everything is meant to make sense in the moment. But God reveals truth over time. He connects the dots. That's how we grow.

Ask Jesus to interfere in your life. Yes, interfere. Let Him send "quality problems" your way. The kind that stretches you, shapes you, and prepares you. The kind that drives out fear. Face your fear and say: *"I will defeat you in Jesus' name."*

Whether it's with your spouse, your kids, or by yourself, walk this out in community. If you don't have a mentor or someone to walk with you, reach out. Email me. Let's connect. That's what this is about: pointing you back to *Him.*

This isn't about me telling you how to run your life. I'm just a voice. You've got choices. But if you want truth. If you want to heal and grow. Open your Bible. If you don't have one, get one. Or download the app. Jesus doesn't want the dedication to law and religion from you. He wants your heart.

I used to think I had to be the "knight in shining armor." I don't anymore. My armor is dented, broken, and battle worn. I've got scars, and they tell a story. *But those scars have been refined by fire.* And now I can offer something real. Not perfection. *Testimony.*

People of all ages go through pain. The question is: How did it shape you? What did you learn? Did you lean on God through it? When you follow Christ, you learn to move forward in *His cadence.* Yeah, I said cadence. It's an actionable word, right? I know I talk real. I even cuss sometimes. So did Peter. And Jesus still *called* him The Rock on which he built his church. Proverbs say a wise person accepts correction. A fool rejects it. Growth requires discipline. Discipline brings growth. God is using me to speak this truth into your life, to help you see that you *can* make it.

You can't do it with your own strength; not for long because human effort drains you. You need the Holy Spirit. You need God's breath in your lungs.

"Worry weighs a person down; an encouraging word lifts them up." - **Proverbs 12:25**.

That's what I'm here to give: a good push. A word of encouragement. Motivation rooted in truth.

WHERE OBEDIENCE BEGINS

"Don't think you are better than you really are. Be honest in your evaluation of yourselves, measuring yourselves by the faith God has given us." - **Romans 12:3 (NLT)**

We often overlook how powerful humility is in our walk with Christ. Being honest with ourselves is one of the hardest, but most necessary, things we can do. Truly look in the mirror and evaluate where you stand in your faith. It's through this kind of reflection that transformation begins.

Lately, I've been spending Monday nights with my men's group, where we open up our minds, study Scripture, and discuss life with honesty. One of the books that has impacted our conversations is *Gospeller* by Willie Robertson. I want to bring pieces of those conversations into this chapter, not only because they've helped shape me, but because they reflect the Holy Spirit working among men who are actively trying to follow Christ in a world full of distractions.

There's something powerful about unity. When a room full of men show their flaws, become vulnerable and gather in honesty, the Spirit shows up. And when the Spirit is present, there's inspiration. Conversations like these aren't just reflections, they are action plans. We go back to our daily lives more equipped to walk in what we believe.

One of the recurring themes that keeps surfacing is this question: *What does it mean to truly follow Jesus?* Not in theory. Not in symbolism. But in action.

We were reading a chapter from *Gospeller* called "Interstellar," and the message hit us square in the chest. One of the guys pointed out a recurring theme: that the Christian life boils down to two things. *Reaching out* and *letting go*. First, we reach outward to others, overflowing with Christ's love. Then, we let go of what holds us back from living that out.

Willie Robertson doesn't hesitate. He sees someone who needs Jesus, and he goes after them. He prays, baptizes, and doesn't waste time worrying whether someone might reject him. For many of us, that boldness can be intimidating. We second guess, we hesitate, and we wonder how people will react. Will they be offended? Will they walk away? But at some point, we must realize we're not responsible for the outcome, only obedience.

Discernment matters. We're not called to push Jesus on people. In fact, aggressive evangelism is what has driven many people *away* from church. But when our hearts are full, when our cup overflows, there comes a time when *we must pour out*. Holding onto that love, keeping it to ourselves, is not the call. Jesus said, "Go." That means *do*.

So, what stops us?

Usually, it's the cost.

The cost of vulnerability. The cost of letting go of control.

"And whoever does not carry their cross and follow me cannot be my disciple" - **Luke 14:27**

The cost of living a new life is the toughest mindset. It reminds us that there is a price to be paid to follow Jesus. And that price? Everything. You must give up your old life. Your habits. Your idols. Even the good things can become idols if they take God's place.

Ask yourself: what's your idol? Prestige? Money? Sexual desire? Relationships? Family? Drugs and Alcohol? Material things like homes or cars?

God may not literally call you to give everything away, but He *does* ask you to lay it all down. To surrender every area of your life to Him. And in doing that, you will find freedom. When you cut the cord to whatever is holding you back, you become lighter. You become open. And that's when your purpose starts to become clear. It starts with trust.

One of the phrases I say often in my own prayer life is this: *"Lord, you have my heart. You have my knee. You have my trust."* That's what He wants. That's all He's ever wanted: *your heart*. From it flows love, the greatest of all the spiritual gifts. Love motivates obedience. Love leads to transformation.

So, if God is asking only for your heart. Why do we make it so complicated?

But the truth is simple: Give Him your heart. Let go of what's holding you back. Step out in faith. We were never called to play it safe. We were called to give it all. Don't forget the greatest gift we have is love.

It won't be easy. But it *will* be worth it.

SURRENDERING THE REIGNS

Many of us want to lean on the law of Moses, like saying, "Well, I don't do this or that, so I'm a good person." But the truth is, we're all still sinners. God knows this, and He's not asking you to be perfect. You won't be perfect, not until you're gone. That's not to discourage you, but to be real with you. Perfection only comes in death.

So don't fear that. The key is trust. Bowing your knee before God, that act of surrender, is giving up your will. It's submitting yourself, whether in pressure-filled moments or times of joy when blessings seem overwhelming. Kneeling before God means saying, "Your will, not mine."

And along with your heart and your surrender, comes trust. Trust that God will place you exactly where you need to be, at the right time, for everything you need in this life. This is praying for wisdom. Wisdom to navigate your path. You might not get there as fast as you'd like, but His timing is perfect.

Patience is tough. We often get frustrated because we're stuck on our own timeline. "Why hasn't it happened yet?

Anxiety builds when you fixate on whatever you're hoping for, whether it's money, family, career, or something else. You want to speed it up, but ironically, it comes quicker when you let God handle it.

Be honest with God. Tell Him your struggles. Maybe you're putting work or possessions above your family. Maybe you work 80 hours a week as a refuge from your responsibilities, but your kids are suffering because you're not there for them. Confess it to God. Vulnerability takes courage, but He already knows anyway. It's about opening your heart and showing your faith, even if your faith feels as small as a mustard seed.

It's about giving God control and letting go of your reins. It might not be a fix where everything suddenly falls into place. Your family won't instantly become perfect, and your struggles won't vanish overnight. But this transformation makes you feel lighter, freer, and braver because you're hearing God's voice and walking in His purpose.

It's okay to be wrong. Too often, arguments stem from who's right or wrong rather than finding a resolution. People cling to opinions, facts, or even scientific data to prove their point, but that's not always what matters. Sometimes, it's about listening, understanding, and respecting the other person's perspective, even if you don't agree.

When conflicts arise, try putting yourself in the other person's shoes. You might not know everything about them, but humility means stepping outside your own viewpoint.

Sometimes resolution takes time. Maybe the other person needs to think things through, and maybe you do, too. That reflection is part of growing.

Take it to God. Ask for guidance, wisdom, and understanding. God will lead you because He is right there with you.

"Many are the woes of the wicked, but the Lord's unfailing love surrounds the one who trust in Him." - **Psalm 32:10**

Remember this, Psalm; it's about repentance and recognizing our true condition. As men, we like to handle things ourselves, but we must learn to surrender those burdens to God. We can't carry it all alone.

Stay in constant prayer, pray without ceasing, as it says. Prayer can be spoken aloud; it can also be silent conversations with the Holy Spirit dwelling inside you. Invite Him into your struggles, your pain, your joys. Let Him carry the weight. And forgiveness. Don't forget to forgive yourself. Let go of bitterness and resentment. The Spirit will lead you on this journey.

"For if you live according to the flesh, you will die; but if by the Spirit you put to death the misdeeds of the body, you will live." - **Romans 8:13**

Romans 8 reminds us we are connected to the Spirit. Through prayer, scripture, service, and fellowship, we build endurance and faith.

[Pastor Mike, Lutheran Church of Hope] Think of yourself as a crockpot, not a microwave. Growth takes time. Patience and persistence lead to real transformation.

CALLED BEYOND FEAR

This morning, I prayed about *bearing the cross*. It ties right into this whole book, about your fears, the things you dread, and what lies beyond them. On the other side of fear is your *purpose*, your *calling*. It's not just something you achieve; it's your anointing, what you were made to do.

And here's the thing, you're not just serving God; you're serving His people. God works through you, and it's not about ego or pride, or bragging rights. This isn't about being appointed to a fancy title. No, this calling brings deep joy and fulfillment because you know, through Him, you've overcome much: depression, trials, and sorrows. Your calling erases those things like Jesus's death erases our sins. It gives you peace.

Why peace? Because you're fulfilling your purpose. You're letting God work through you. And when that happens, your aura shines. The people God placed in your life feel that light and it makes them better too. This is the beauty of serving.

Sure, we can get moments of pride, maybe from sports achievements or a job promotion, but those things don't sustain us like God's peace does. When you embrace your calling with selflessness, your anointing impacts not just you, but the world around you. It can be as simple as a friendly "hi," a deep conversation, or even a tough debate that leads to resolution. I've heard it described as *"the anointing comes before the appointing"*. The call and the commission. Those words are so close, but the anointing always comes first, preparing you for what is next.

Back to *bearing the cross*: at first, it sounds brave. You think, "I'm ready. I'm taking this risk with God." But then, BAM! Life hits you hard. That's the slap that wakes you up. You realize this isn't about pride or ego; you must check those at the door. That's part of bearing the cross.

And don't expect to get it all right in one day. We're humans, and we like the idea of living out our entire journey in a single day, like a movie. A good friend of mine once told me, "Movies are life with the boring parts cut out." But life isn't a movie. It's a process. The first step tests your courage: will you back down and return to mediocrity, or will you keep moving forward?

Some of us settle for mediocrity, but most of us feel the pull for more. Maybe your dreams didn't come true because of injury, money, trauma, or loss. The question is: are you playing victim or moving forward? Do you still have that fighting spirit?

I can relate. I chased a music dream for years, playing clarinet, drums, guitar, hoping to be a musician or teacher. But I never fully committed. I gave up on that dream, realizing maybe it wasn't my calling. That "wasted time" taught me something: it prepared me for where I am now. You might have tried many things that didn't work out. Maybe you wanted to be a model, learn a language, or something different. Those failures? They're not setbacks. They're the roadmap to your true path.

When you bear your cross, all those trials, dreams, and lessons align. Your hardships aren't meaningless; they are the preparation for your calling.

So, wherever you are now, pick up your cross and follow Him. Take the risk. Dream big. God wants you to dream big. He wants you to take risks, even fail. That's what bearing the cross is about. You took the first step and got smacked down by pride or ego. Now, will you return to God and say, "I'm all in, no matter what"? That's what God wants. To seek Him daily. To rely on Him and expect His promises.

If your prayers aren't answered overnight, keep trusting Him. Praise Him for the opportunities in the day and expect miracles tomorrow. And if anxiety and stress creep in, let it go. Give it to God. He's got the big stuff covered. You just need faith.

God sees your heart and wants you to come to Him with everything. Your struggles, dreams, and hopes. He's not looking for perfect effort, but for your heart. Yes, you must work, go to school, and care for your family. But prayer and faith mean believing *as if it's already done*. Pray like you've already graduated, already been healed, or already received that blessing.

We weren't meant to just work 40 hours a week. To clock in and out and settle for a mediocre life. That is a manufactured system. We are creators. Made to imagine, to build, to love, and to nurture. Man and woman were created as partners. To create and protect the next generation, raising them in faith. Following God and bearing your cross isn't scary, it's a journey. Life will bring trials and sorrows, but with faith, you can navigate them.

I'm not perfect. I'm just sharing what I've learned on the other side of hardships. Maybe you've faced greater trials? What matters is what you do in those moments. What can God teach you? What can you carry forward?

I promise you; you are on the right path. God has a plan for you. He gives you free will to navigate it, but He is always there, guiding you through the challenges you'd rather avoid. So, take Him up on His offer. Come to Him. He wants to reveal your purpose. Your calling. Your anointing.

Go after your dreams. Take up your cross. Follow Christ.

CREATED WITH PURPOSE

I was on my way to church and feeling inspired to share some thoughts with you. Recently, I bought my dream acreage. This morning, I felt strengthened by the Lord. Strong, mighty, and valiant like Gideon and David. I'm a masterpiece created in God's image, just like you are.

God works through all of us, but we must open ourselves to His Spirit. Your desires should be genuine and centered on purpose, not just personal pleasure, but on how your gifts can serve others. True fulfillment is the action of creating relationships and bringing those people to heaven. Relationships are our treasures.

If you're a motivator or someone who shares encouragement, remember you're not just receiving motivation, you're sharing it and blessing others with your testimony. Not everyone will appreciate it, some might even resist or doubt you, but that's okay. If you're fighting through darkness, hold on. For those seeking hope, know that God is working to reach you today.

We all share a human experience. Pain. Struggles. Victories. But each journey is unique. If you haven't yet, invite God into your heart. Ask Him to reveal your gifts and your calling. Everyone has a destiny, man or woman, and it's something to be proud of. But don't chase after fame or secondary rewards, like beauty or popularity. True purpose is deeper than that.

For example, many people want to be influencers or life coaches these days. That's fine but be mindful about why you're pursuing it. Is it for attention or to truly help others? Your impact is about authenticity, not surface appeal. And remember, what works for others may not work for you. Find your own path.

Your purpose may or may not align with your career, it might be something you do on the side. God supports all of it. Even in tough times, you can find peace by staying true to yourself and trusting Him. Isolation isn't loneliness when God is with you. Now, I want to talk about the person you are now, and the person God designed you to be. Your spirit existed before you came to this earth, full of wisdom and strength. You agreed to come here, to start fresh and learn through human experience. It's a challenge, but your life is amazing because every struggle teaches you to rely on God. We can't do this alone. I get to give my life to God daily to live in His spirit. You must do the same. Close the gap between who you are now and who God intended you to be. In demanding times, say, "God, make me better day by day," and stick to that path.

There is a daily battle between the spirit and the flesh. Deny the flesh by fasting, not because food is bad, but to show that it does not control you. You can replace food with any other distraction. It could be social media, alcohol, or gambling. Your real nourishment comes from God's spirit. Also, life will pull you between two mindsets: serious responsibility and relaxed enjoyment. Both are inside you, constantly fighting for attention. Finding balance is a lifelong struggle. Sometimes you will lean one way, sometimes the other. Stay mindful, so distractions don't throw you off course.

This reminds me of a '90s movie called *Airborne*. It's about a teenager facing new challenges and learning to balance seriousness with fun.

"You're not afraid of guys like that, are you? The louder they yell, the less dangerous they usually are. I've known a lot of them. There was one guy, a real tough surfer, who would fight anyone who got near "his" wave. One day, he went after a kid on a boogie board, just trying to scare him off. But he got too close, and the skegs from his board cut into the kid's head. Blood everywhere. The kid nearly drowned. He lived, but with a scar that told the story." [*Mitchell Goosen – Airborne 1993*]

The lesson? "You spend so much time fighting over waves that you never enjoy the ocean. Life's too precious for that." [*Mitchell Goosen – Airborne 1993*] You only get one shot, why not enjoy it? Let go of control and let God handle the rest.

Later in the movie, Jack and Mitchell clash. Both want to be the protector—Jack as the overprotective brother, Mitchell as Nikki's new boyfriend. But their styles are opposite. Jack is loud, provoking, trying to scare and intimidate. Mitchell is calm, laid back, even joking. It's like two voices in our own heads: one side is tough, hungry for a fight; the other side is experienced, already been through it, not interested in wasting energy on the wrong battles.

That's what the movie captures, real life. At school, competition is constant. Bullies come in all forms: broke or wealthy, jocks or preps. It's all the same game of status and proving yourself. Jack is desperate to prove he's worth something. Deep down, though, bullies are just looking for love, even if they'll never admit it.

Mitchell, for his part, tries to stay cool, but Jack pushes too far. He taunts, takes off his jacket, sizes him up, trying to awaken that anger inside him. Mitchell fires back, but in his emotions, he says something that hurts Nikki, he claims he doesn't care about anyone because he's leaving in three months. He didn't mean it that way. What he really meant was: *Jack, I'm not playing your game. I won't take the bait. Your fight isn't worth it.*

That ties back to what he told Nikki earlier: nothing here is worth fighting for. Because in the end, when Mitchell's gone, Jack will just find someone else to battle. That's the paradox of hate; it never ends until someone chooses to stop feeding it.

You'll relate whether you're young or grown. The takeaway? Love one another, even when conflict arises. People come into your life for a reason, some challenge you to grow, even if they seem like "bullies." Seek to understand them and find peace in God's plan.

Your trials are growth opportunities. Don't run from pain or hardship. Embrace them, learn, and allow them to strengthen you. You'll face every emotion; anger, sadness, frustration and that's okay. Through it all, you'll find strength in God's love. Remember, we're human, and we try to understand the supernatural with logic, it won't always make sense. Trust God anyway. He's working for you, even when you can't see it. Live in the present. Don't dwell on the past or worry excessively about the future. Learn from yesterday but focus on today. Walk with God step by step.

I love you all, and I pray this book reaches you when you need it most. May God bless you on your journey to becoming who you were meant to be. In Jesus' name, Amen.

THE COURAGE TO MOVE

I've been looking back at some of my notes on fear, and one thing really stuck out: you can't overcome fear just through positive experiences. Life expands and contracts according to the courage you show when you're in pain. You've got to be willing to stand up to fear. You've got to sort through your life and make peace with the fact that there's never an easy time to make a hard decision. Never. But that doesn't mean the decision isn't necessary.

You've got nothing to be afraid of. Fear paralyzes, and the more you delay, the more power it gains. I read somewhere that self-esteem is mostly formed in the first seven or eight years of your life. Think about that. Some of us had a lack of role models, a lack of structure, and a lack of love. That's where the damage started. That's why it's so hard to rebuild. But that's also why we've got to take action now. You don't just level up by sitting in the same spot. Sometimes, in order to grow closer to Him, God will take a relationship away from you. He'll remove that comfort, so you draw closer to Him. He's not punishing you. He's promoting you.

God always has something better—always. He's not in the business of breaking you without rebuilding you. You are a work in progress. I am a work in progress. And if you're in the middle of something painful right now, it could be because He's preparing you to learn something new through Him. You're about to level up. And let me tell you something: where God is taking you, not everybody can follow. They're not supposed to. That calling on your life? That battle? It's spiritual. It's massive. And it's yours.

You want to know if you're really living your faith? Check your actions. Does your lifestyle match what you claim to believe? I'm not asking for perfection, we can't give that. I'm talking about movement. Momentum. Growth. Let your light shine through your actions, not just your words.

Here's where it gets real: the hardest things I've ever done? Those were the most meaningful. The most transformative. That's where truth lives—in the hardest thing you're willing to face. You want to find what's real? Go after the hardest challenge in your life. Run toward it, not away from it. [*Jordan Peterson – The Shawn Ryan Show*]

The Bible is the truth. The Holy Spirit uses it like a map for your future. But you won't see that vision clearly until you take action. You've got to orient your life around the Word if you want to become the person God created you to be. Then you must look directly at what terrifies you. Don't shrink back. Don't retreat into the dark. Practice speaking the truth over yourself, about who you are, and who He says you are. Speak it into your existence. Walk in it.

That means vulnerability. That means courage. That means taking a risk. I've been preaching that for a while now, and I stand by it. You've got to be willing to live in the light—even though the darkness feels familiar. That's why abuse feels comfortable. That's why dysfunction feels like home. Because we've gotten used to it. It's what we know.

But that darkness? It's not the truth. It's a trap. It's comfort without growth. It's control without faith. The light takes effort. The light demands your heart. It requires your vulnerability—your raw, real self. But the light is where transformation lives.

Sometimes, you get something new and real right in front of you—an opportunity, a blessing, and you're scared of it. Not because it's bad, but because it's unfamiliar. Because you start trying to connect it to your past trauma. You start creating stories in your mind about how this will go wrong like it did before. You're pulling from a past pain that doesn't even belong in this chapter of your life.

And here's the crazy part: sometimes the very thing you're running from is the thing God has sent to bless you. But you're too scared to receive it because you're still listening to those old stories. You're still living in a loop. It's time to break the pattern.

You've got to face it. You've got to go right at it. Hit your demon head-on. Face your Goliath. And don't be scared. Why? Because you've got God. The Holy Spirit is your strength. You've got the full armor: the helmet of salvation, the breastplate of righteousness, the belt of truth, the shoes of peace, the shield of faith, and the sword of the Spirit. But what covers your back? God. That's right—God's got your back. So, move forward. Take the step. He's not going to let fall.

This is why it's so hard. This is what you're afraid of: forward movement, and the unknown. That's what's got you stuck. You're still looking back. Still obsessing over what happened. Still living in the shame of your past. Stop letting that pain define you.

Here's the truth: somebody hurt you. Maybe they humiliated you. Maybe they abandoned you. And now, you are carrying that weight, hoping no one else sees it. You're embarrassed. You're exhausted. But listen to me—who cares what they think? Who are they to rank your value?

You are not what happened to you. You are not the lie that shame keeps repeating in your mind. You are a child of God. And that's the only identity that matters. Let go of what you can't control. Do your part and trust God with the rest. Stop worrying about tomorrow. Matthew 6:34 says, "So don't worry about tomorrow, for tomorrow will bring its own worries. Today's trouble is enough for today." That verse is real life.

And Isaiah 54:17 reminds us: "No weapon formed against you will prosper." I've lived that. You've lived that. Every single one of us has been through something that should have destroyed us—but we're still here. That's not luck. That's grace.

The fear you're feeling. That fear that keeps you frozen? It's not just fear of failure. It's fear of pain. Of judgment. Of being seen. But guess what? You've already been through worse. And you're still standing. So, move forward. Press in. Seek God's voice, not the crowd's opinion. You don't need their approval. You need His presence.

Now, let's talk about the growth that comes after facing fear—what I call leveling up. It's like a video game. Level one? You're just learning how to move. Learning to jump, to duck, to fight. You face your first boss, and it might take a couple of tries, but you figure it out. Why? Because you've studied it. And every level after that gets harder.

But you grow. You gain knowledge. You gain experience. By the time you get to level ten, all the old enemies return—but now you're prepared. You've seen their tactics. You've learned your skills. You've developed discernment. And even when you face the final boss—the unknown—you're not afraid anymore. Why? Because God has trained you for this.

You are stronger now. Wiser. Disciplined. Because you stayed in the fight.

I've been crushed before, broken down to nothing. But I didn't die. The enemy tried, but God wouldn't let me go. And I asked for this. I asked Jesus to interfere in my life. I asked Him to make it hard so I could grow. I wanted strong shoulders to carry a heavy burden. I wanted to be courageous like David. Like Gideon. And you know what? He answered.

Now I'm going through another storm. But this time, I know how to handle it. Because I've been through the fire, and I came out refined. So maybe you're in your storm right now. Maybe you're crushed. But you're not done. You're not finished. You're in the middle of your training. Let God develop you. Let Him grow you. Let Him show you what's on the other side of your fear.

Because your destiny is waiting. Just walk through the door. And don't look back.

WHEN FEAR WHISPERS

There's something strange about the quiet moments. You know the ones I'm talking about—the in-between hours, the moments after a conversation that left you uneasy, the late nights when the world falls silent, and your thoughts suddenly grow loud. It's in those moments that fear doesn't just whisper, it roars. It replays conversations, imagines catastrophes, reminds you of failures, and convinces you that something worse is coming. And somehow, even when nothing has happened, fear convinces you that everything is falling apart.

But here's the thing: fear talks loudest when it knows faith is nearby.

Let that sink in. When you're on the edge of growth, when you're stepping into something new, when you've prayed and committed to walking in purpose, fear gets desperate. It scrambles for your attention because it knows faith is about to take the wheel. Fear wants to stop you before you remember who walks beside you.

That's the fight. Not just the external pressures, but the internal battle to choose faith when fear is throwing a tantrum. And believe me, fear will throw everything at you: memories, lies, doubt, embarrassment, guilt, anxiety—all of it. It doesn't play fairly. It uses your past and tries to hijack your future. But this is where we get stronger. Not because we magically eliminate fear, but because we learn how to stop bowing to it.

Some people think being faithful means walking around like everything is fine all the time, but faith doesn't mean you don't feel fear. It means you don't obey it or don't allow it to consume you.

Fear does not always show up screaming. Sometimes it shows up reasonable. It sounds like caution. Like wisdom. Like being "realistic." It tells you to slow down, to wait a little longer, to make sure you're ready. And on the surface, none of that sounds dangerous. But underneath it all, fear has one goal: delay obedience long enough that you talk yourself out of it. Fear rarely tells you to quit outright. It just asks you to hesitate.

At some point, every person of faith reaches a moment where knowing isn't the problem anymore. The issue isn't clarity — it's courage. It's the moment when God says, "Move," and fear responds with, "But what if?"

What if you fail?

What if you look foolish?

What if it costs more than you thought?

Fear thrives in that space between instruction and action. Here is the truth we don't like admitting:

Most spiritual stagnation isn't rebellion. It's procrastination.

We keep waiting for peace before we obey when peace usually comes after obedience. We want guarantees before movement, confirmation before commitment. But faith does not work that way. Faith moves first — clarity follows. I've had moments where I knew exactly what God was asking of me, and I still stalled. Not because I didn't believe Him, but because I didn't trust myself to survive the discomfort of obedience. Fear wasn't questioning God's faithfulness — it was questioning my capacity. That's a dangerous place to stay.

Because fear will let you stay busy. It will let you stay spiritual. It will let you keep talking about purpose — as long as you don't actually step into it. It will disguise disobedience as patience and call avoidance "waiting on the Lord. But eventually, faith demands a decision. There comes a moment when you have to stop negotiating with fear and start exercising authority over it. Not emotionally. Spiritually. You don't argue with fear — you interrupt it. You remind it who's in charge. You move even while your hands are shaking. Courage isn't the absence of fear. It is acting while fear is still in the room.

Some of the most faithful steps I've ever taken were uncomfortable, unglamorous, and misunderstood. They didn't come with applause or instant results. But they came with alignment. And alignment changes everything. When you move in obedience, even imperfectly, you step into momentum that fear cannot sustain. Fear is loud at the starting line. It's quiet once you start moving.

That's because fear feeds on imagination, not action. It survives on "what ifs," not follow-through. The moment you take the step, fear loses leverage. It may not disappear, but it no longer has control.

And maybe that's what this season is really about for you.

Permission to move. You don't need to feel ready. You need to be willing. Faith doesn't wait for perfect conditions. It responds to divine instruction. And when you finally move — not confidently, but obediently — you will realize something powerful: God had already gone ahead of you. Fear never stood a chance.

Real faith is raw. It's honest. It says, "Yes, I'm scared. Yes, I'm unsure. But I trust the One who sees further than I do." Faith is not loud; sometimes, it's a whisper. Sometimes it's just holding on by a thread. But it holds on.

And maybe that's where you are right now, just holding on. Maybe you've been putting on a brave face while everything inside you is screaming. You're tired. You're discouraged. You've prayed, and you're still waiting. You've read the Word, but it feels like it's not sinking in. You see people around you are succeeding while you're stuck wondering if your breakthrough got lost in the mail.

But I need to tell you this: the silence doesn't mean God isn't moving.

Faith often grows in quiet soil. You don't see roots forming underground, but that doesn't mean they aren't there. Sometimes God is building the foundation for something greater, and all you're being asked to do is *not give up*. That's it. Just hold on. Take one more step. Not because fear is gone, but because you are no longer giving it permission to lead.

I remember a season when I thought I had everything I ever prayed for. I could see it. I could taste it. But then it slipped away, almost overnight. It left me stunned. And fear came in like a flood, whispering, "You're not good enough. This is why things never work out. You will never recover from this." Do you ever hear those kinds of lies? The kind that sounds like truth because they wear the clothes of your past.

But in that space, I learned something life changing. I learned how to sit in the presence of God when nothing made sense. I learned that He doesn't require me to have answers, only trust. And that's what I gave Him, one hour at a time, then one day at a time. It was slow, and it was painful. But it was also holy.

You see, faith doesn't guarantee a fast result. It guarantees a firm anchor. We want instant gratification, without patience for things to marinate. You won't be tossed around every time a storm rolls in because you've learned to be still. You've learned to listen. You've learned to trust that God is writing a story bigger than your setback, stronger than your struggle, and deeper than your doubts.

This is how you resist fear: not by pretending it doesn't exist, but by choosing who gets the final word. And that final word belongs to God. It always has. So today, maybe all you need is a reminder: you're still in the story. Fear didn't win. It may have knocked you around, but it didn't get the victory. You're still here. Still praying. Still hoping. Still showing up.

That is faith. And I promise you—God honors that.

WHERE TWO OR MORE ARE CALLED

Sometimes we need to remind ourselves that we were never meant to walk this journey alone. That's part of what makes faith so powerful, it's not just believing in God when life is good but trusting Him when everything feels like it's falling apart. And one of the biggest ways to stay rooted in that faith is through community, connection, and the power of the Holy Spirit guiding us from within.

Being in a church community changed everything for me. Surrounding yourself with like-minded people isn't about fellowship, it's spiritual reinforcement. Remember what the Bible says: *"Where two or more are gathered, there I am with them." Matthew 18:20*. That means the Holy Spirit is right there in the midst of us. You're not just attending a service; you're stepping into a spiritual battleground where your faith gets sharpened, your heart gets fed, and your soul gets strengthened.

And the Holy Spirit is not just beside you; He's within you. That voice in your conscience that steers you, that nudges you toward truth and conviction, that's Him. He doesn't speak on His own; He speaks what He hears from the Father. And what He hears is truth. That's why it's crucial to stay in the Word. If you want to know what the Holy Spirit is saying to you, go back to your Bible. Read it and soak it all up.

Let me say this plainly: God, Jesus, and the Holy Spirit are three distinct persons, but one united Trinity. I'm not diving deep into theological breakdowns here but understand this; Jesus died for you, and when He ascended into heaven, He sent the Advocate: Holy Spirit. That's who walks with you now. He will be with you until your last breath when you finally meet your Savior face to face. If you haven't already, ask Jesus into your life. Say something like this: "Jesus, I believe **you** died for my sins. I believe **you** rose from the grave. I believe **you're** alive and reigning in heaven, and I want to give my life to **you**. Save me. Forgive me. Lead me. I want to live eternally with **you**."

This isn't just a one-time decision. It's a lifelong transformation. Turning from sin, walking away from the ways of the world, and clinging to the truth of Christ. The Bible isn't just a book—it's your compass. And the Holy Spirit is your inner guide. Lean on Him. Talk to Him. Invite Him into every decision, every doubt, every valley.

Another way to deepen your faith is through service. Volunteering opens a part of your heart that nothing else can. Whether it's ushering, greeting, helping the homeless. I serve by working traffic control at my church. It builds something eternal. It connects my gifts to God's purpose.

Let me say this: working traffic control might seem small, but it's one of the greatest joys I've experienced. There's purpose in the seemingly simple. When you serve others, your faith expands. You feel alive. You feel aligned.

And faith isn't just something you feel, it's something you hold onto in the dark. Psalm 56:3–4 says it perfectly: *"But when I am afraid, I will put my trust in You... What can mere mortals do to me?"* Think about that. What can people really do to you when you've got God? Your circumstances aren't permanent. They're temporary trials that God will walk you through, if you let Him.

Hebrews 11:1 puts it plainly: *"Faith shows the reality of what we hope for; it is the evidence of things we cannot see."* Faith is believing before the breakthrough. It's trusting without having all the answers.

Let me share something personal. I had a relationship that didn't work out. It was painful, and I had to grieve not just the person, but the future I had imagined. But that season forced me to anchor myself in God. I sought counseling and therapy. I leaned into community. I started working out, not just for my body but for a new mindset and discipline. I journaled. I wrote down scriptures, hung them on my wall. I listened to Joel Osteen when I needed to feel hope. I watched Steven Furtick when I needed spiritual fire. I found my rhythm within Christ. My daily walk with God was no longer something I turned to just in pain, but something I lived by in peace.

And even now, I speak my future into existence. I walk by faith, not by sight. I declare that I'm going to live in my dream home. I'm going to meet the wife God has for me. I'm going to raise the family He's promised. Why? Because the Lord has already written it. I encourage you to do the same. Speak life over your situation. Don't wait until everything looks perfect. Faith isn't about appearances, it's about truth. Truth in the One who created you, redeemed you, and walks beside you now.

Proverbs 3:5–6 says, *"Trust in the Lord with all your heart and do not lean on your own understanding. In all your ways acknowledge Him, and He will make your paths straight."* That's a promise. Not a maybe. Not a "we'll see." That's a guarantee.

So, whatever you are walking through remember, fear doesn't get the final word. Faith does.

Speak it. Walk it. Believe it.

You've got this. Not because you're strong, but because your God is.

HOPE AND A FUTURE

Sometimes, life feels like a big mess. Like you're stuck in a pile of confusion, fear, and questions. And that's okay, because that's often where we start before God begins to reveal His plan for us.

The Bible talks about destiny in a way that's so powerful and comforting. God's destiny for you is not random or chaotic. It's a divine plan carefully laid out and perfectly timed. Jeremiah 29:11 is one of my favorite promises from the Lord.

"For I know the plans I have for you," declares the Lord, "plans to prosper you and not to harm you, plans to give you hope and a future."

That verse isn't just a nice quote to hang on your wall, it's a powerful reminder that God has a good plan for your life, even when things don't feel good.

God's not some cosmic puppeteer who throws us around for His entertainment. No, He's sovereign, meaning He is in control, loving, and intentional. He has designed a path for each of us, and when we align ourselves with Him, we begin to walk in joy and fulfillment. And here's the thing, sometimes we use the wrong words to describe that pursuit. We say "chase" when it comes to dreams, goals, or even relationships. But chasing feels frantic, exhausting, like going after something that's running away from you. Pursuing, on the other hand, means you're following a path that's meant for you; steady, hopeful, confident. (Note to all men, you should be pursuing your wife, not chasing her.)

When you're pursuing God's destiny for you, things will begin to fall into place. You won't be exhausted from trying to force it. Your relationships, your purpose, and your goals will align because God's plan is always for your good. It's not magic or a fairy tale, but spiritual and supernatural. It lights a fire inside of you, a fire of peace, passion, and purpose. It brings out the best version of yourself, the person you were meant to be.

But here's the challenge: you have free will. God gave you the freedom to choose, to decide your own steps. Sometimes you might veer off the path. Sometimes you might feel lost or hurt. But even in those moments, God's plan is still at work. He's not surprised by your detours or your doubts. He's patient and loving, guiding you back when you're ready to trust Him again.

That trust is what matters most. It's surrendering your heart, your will, and your faith to Him. Imagine it like this: you give God your heart; that is, your love and your true desires. You give Him your knee; that's your surrender, your willingness to bow to His plan, even when it's hard. And you give Him your trust; your faith to believe that He is working everything out for your good, even when you can't see it.

When you give your heart, knee, and trust to God, you unlock a peace that the world can't offer. Your destiny isn't just a vague idea; it's a living promise rooted in God's wisdom and love. It unfolds at the right time and in the right way, shaped by His hand.

And remember, every person God places in your life is part of that destiny. Friends, family, even strangers, they all serve a purpose. Sometimes they teach you lessons; sometimes you help guide them. Sometimes they are with you for a season, other times for a lifetime. But none of it is accidental. Each connection is part of God's divine plan to shape you and your journey.

When you feel broken, hurt, or at your lowest, remember that God hears you. *"Then you will call on me and come and pray to me, and I will listen to you. You will seek me and find me when you seek me with all your heart. I will be found by you."* - **Jeremiah 29:12-14**

God is not distant. He wants you to pour your heart out to Him. Cry out and be honest with your pain and fears. He listens because He loves you deeply.

Just like King David, who cried out to God through years of struggle, you are not alone. You may feel banished, broken, or lost, but God promises to bring you back. He gathers you from any place where you feel scattered or hurt. His plans for you are to restore, prosper, and fill you with hope.

That hope isn't just for the future in heaven, though that is the ultimate promise; it's for today. It's the strength to keep going, the peace to trust Him through the storms, and the courage to pursue the path He's laid before you. Sustainability in His strength, not yours. You weren't meant to tackle everyday life in your own strength. You can't do it without his help.

Your destiny is waiting. It's not about chasing something out of reach. It's about walking steadily in faith, surrendering your heart, and trusting the God who loves you perfectly. So, take a deep breath. Let go of fear and chaos. Open your heart to God's plan. Pursue your destiny with faith, because He is already ahead of you, preparing the way.

HARNESSING THE HOLY SPIRIT

One of the ideas that keeps coming up is harnessing the power of the Holy Spirit. I know we've touched on that before in this book, but it's one of those things that deserves repeating. Because it's deeper than we think.

Here's a thought from the Spirit: A bully acts out in evil, not always because they're mean, but because they've been hurt. Deeply. A bully feels like they've been robbed of everything. Stripped of dignity. Maybe of love. Maybe of security. And now they move through life with pride. Not the healthy kind, but the kind that refuses to let anyone else win. Especially not in front of others. It's like they crave a stage to act out their pain and walk with a puffed-up chest.

And that's where Satan loves to play. He whispers, "Let the world see your pain. Make them pay for not protecting you." But here's the truth: that's not justice. That's not healing. That's just recycled hate. That's not strength. That's bondage.

Now let's circle back to the Holy Spirit.

See, when you've got all these bad thoughts flooding your mind, when your head's spinning with what they said or did, and when it's hard to even breathe without anger rising, you don't fight that in your own power. You ask the Spirit to step in. Now, let's be clear: the Spirit is already in you if you've repented and accepted salvation through Christ. But you've got to give Him access. Surrender control. Ask Him to capture every thought. Catch every emotion before it turns into poison.

The Holy Spirit is God's presence in you. He's not just floating around like a nice idea. He's active. Alive. Powerful. And He hears everything—both from God and from you. He is the one who reminds you of God's Word, the truth. He is the one who gives you discernment. He is the one who convicts and comforts at the same time.

"But the Advocate, the Holy Spirit, whom my Father will send in my name, will teach you all things and will remind you of everything I have said to you." - **John 14:26**

But when he, the Spirit of truth comes, he will guide you into all the truth. He will not speak on his own; he will speak only what he hears, and he will tell you what is to come. - **John 16:13**

Jesus said God would send the Advocate, the Spirit of truth, and that this Spirit would speak not on His own, but only what He hears from the Father. He would tell us what is yet to come. That's power. That's clarity. That's supernatural guidance. And my man Paul was the human advocate for this. He lived and breathed and wrote the message. He wasn't just out there preaching. He was out there bleeding for the Gospel. He penned it so we could read it, understand it, and apply it.

Now I want to say this as plainly as I can: if you're not harnessing the power of the Holy Spirit, then you are running on fumes. You are drained. The enemy will circle like a vulture waiting for a moment of weakness. But the beautiful paradox is this: in your weakness, God's strength is revealed. Don't let the devil have your thoughts. Don't let him convince you that your depression, your rage, your disappointment are permanent. He's a liar. And not just any liar, he is the original.

Satan is a sore loser. Think about it. He was in heaven. He had beauty. Power. Position. But he got prideful. He wanted to be God. So, he got kicked out. And ever since then, he's been throwing a tantrum like a child who didn't get his way. He's not some equal rival to God. He's not this powerful being standing toe-to-toe with the Almighty. No. He's a disgraced creation acting out of bitterness and jealousy.

Imagine it like this: the whistle blows at the end of the Super Bowl. One team wins. But the losing team refuses to leave the field. They throw helmets. They knock over the trophy. They curse out the MVP. That's Satan. He lost. But he's still on the field causing chaos and trying to ruin the celebration. But here's the wild part: he's not just throwing a fit for himself. He's recruiting. He's whispering lies into people's ears, getting them to join in his tantrum. Making them think they've been cheated out of life, too. Making them believe their pain is their identity.

And that's where the bully comes in. Most bullies aren't born cruel. They're made. Somewhere along the way, someone failed them. Someone ignored their pain. Someone made them feel invisible. And now they act out that pain by making others feel small. Because they think hurting you might somehow heal them.

But here's the truth: love beats hate. Every time. Hate can't beat hate. It creates more. That's why shouting matches on Facebook are meaningless. You're not solving anything. You're just adding gasoline to the fire. No matter what you say in the comments, it's never enough. It's infinite noise. There is no such thing as a "mic drop." Evil isn't looking for a final word. No, instead it whispers in everyone's ear to "get their word in." Go ahead. It will be ok. You'll be the one to end it and everyone will clap for you. What you don't realize is Satan is telling everyone else that as well. It's a diabolical paradox of pure hate that robs you of your energy.

But love. Love disarms. Love says, "I see your pain, but I won't match your anger. I'm here to understand your hurt." That's what changes things. That's how Jesus lived. That's what He calls us to do.

Now, this doesn't mean you let people run over you. You need wisdom, discernment and boundaries. Some people are not safe to be around. Some people are not your assignment. But you can still pray for them. You can still release the bitterness. You can still let go of the offense so that their darkness doesn't infect your light.

And, just maybe, you find out what's really hurting that person. What's the root? What lie have they believed? What wound have they been nursing for years? If you can love someone through that, without getting trapped or used, then you're walking in His Kingdom. That's how Spirit works. He gives you the vision to see deeper than behavior. He shows you pain beneath pride. He teaches you how to respond, not to react.

Satan throws tantrums. Christ responds with truth.

So, here's my challenge to you: Don't join the enemy's pity party. Don't throw a fit in response to his. Stand in your authority as a child of God. Invite the Spirit into your thoughts. Let Him lead you. Let Him help you see people the way Jesus sees them. And when you come across someone full of hate, pray. God will lead you to love them anyway.

Because this world doesn't need more noise. It needs more light. Fight from victory. Take action. Shine on.

HKT

ANCHORED IN TRUTH

In order to be strong, you've got to admit where you're weak. Read it again. Not when, but where. Find where your weakness resides. But here's the thing, not all weaknesses are meant to be conquered. Some of them are meant to stay. I'm not saying that we should embrace sin or remain stagnant, but to understand that we're not perfect. They remind us that we're both sinners and humans. And no matter how much discipline we apply, we're never going to turn every weakness into a strength. I've had to learn this the hard way. We talk a lot about turning weakness into strength and sure, there's truth in that. But the deeper truth is some weaknesses stick around. They humble us. We need God's help for this daily battle.

We're not perfect. Not even close. And this is okay. So, we are not going to flip every flaw into a superpower. That's just not real life. That's motivational fluff that forgets what it means to wrestle with the flesh. Instead, we've got to do something harder: we've got to walk with both. We can't do this alone. What we can do, though, is pair our strengths and our weaknesses together. Use our weaknesses not as shame, but as fuel. As discipline. We allow it to humble, motivate, and remind us of our need for God's grace. We're not always going to be running at full strength. Life will knock us down. That's why I look at life as a pattern of mountains and valleys. You have one mountain, a valley, then another mountain, and yet another valley. Over and over again until the day we're gone. It's an endurance race.

You're never going to reach a place in this life where you've beat *every* struggle. You're not going to wake up one day and be immune to fear, to temptation, to insecurity, or to pride. That's not how it works. Life is built on small moments. When stitched together with patience and faith those small moments create something meaningful. Something eternal. He wants you to manage the small blessings, so you know how to oversee the bigger blessings when it's time.

One moment, you're climbing. The next, you're falling. Then you're resting in the middle, looking back at where you came from and looking up at what's still ahead. And just when you reach the top again, there's another challenge. Another lesson. This cycle doesn't stop until we're gone from this world.

Let me put it like this: the goal is to hold onto 5,000 things in your brain, putting together the pieces of your life like a puzzle, and having the patience to let it grow and change. This book is a launchpad. It's about speaking life into yourself and others. It's about getting on the offense, taking action in every area of your life, not out of fear of rejection, but out of resilience and bold faith.

Even the small things you're doing right now are shaping you. Right now, you're learning. Even if you've made mistakes. Even if your past is messy. It's not wasted. What matters is what you do *with* it. Can you learn and move forward with intention? That's what living in the moment really is. Being aware. Paying attention. Showing up. Staying teachable.

And when it comes to relationships, especially the kind that are supposed to last, you're not just building chemistry. You're building a foundation. But if you're always changing who you are to please someone or keep up with trends, then you're building your house on sand. That's why everything eventually collapses. Because attention-seeking isn't the same as purpose-building and you will always find that in Christ.

So many people want to be seen. They want the world to revolve around their pain, their story, and their desires. Let me be honest, this world doesn't revolve around you. Your feelings, your image, your aesthetic, none of that is what makes you matter. It revolves around God. And until we realize that we're going to keep building houses that fall apart in the storm.

If your whole mindset is self-empowerment, this idea that you're the center of your universe, and everyone else should orbit around your trauma, your narrative, your needs, then you're not building the Kingdom. You're building a shrine for yourself. God sees you. God knows you. God loves you. And that's enough. But if your sense of worth is tied up in likes, clicks, reposts, or clout, you're going to starve spiritually. You'll be running a race that leads nowhere.

Hear me out on this: you can't build anything real if you're constantly changing your foundation. If you're always reinventing yourself, always moving the goalposts, always shifting identities to fit the crowd or the moment, then you're building your house on sand. And Scripture tells us the outcome when the storm hits; your house falls and crashes because nothing was anchored. Too many people today are obsessed with change, but not the kind that leads to growth. Not transformation but wasted motion. It's all noise. It's constantly changing for the sake of attention. For validation. It's the kind of change that screams, "Look at me! Pay attention to *me!*" But real change doesn't beg for attention. It builds quietly. It strengthens over time. It serves others.

I've seen it play out at work too. It doesn't matter if it's a restaurant, an office, or a warehouse. Every job has the same type of people. The ones who call in sick every week. The ones who always show up. The ones who cut corners. The ones who carry the weight. The ones who are dependable and the ones who disappear. We're all on different paths, different stories, and different timelines.

And I say that with love, not condemnation. Because we've all been there. We've all had moments of entitlement, ego, and pride. We are maturing when we step outside ourselves and put others before us. Step outside yourself and put others before you. Listen. Serve. Be present.

That is how real purpose is lived out. That's how lives are changed. I know I've only scratched the surface here, and I probably didn't capture everything I thought about this morning, but this is a good start.

Hold onto your strengths. Acknowledge your weaknesses. Don't run from them, learn from them. Don't try to build your life around the applause of others, build it on the solid ground of truth, integrity, and faith. Because when the valleys hit, and they *will*, you'll need something deeper to stand on than just an image. You'll need God. He will be there.

.

WALKING WITHOUT A MAP

I was thinking deeply about confidence, about knowing which direction to go in life. The truth is, sometimes you won't know. Sometimes you're standing at a crossroads and both ways are foggy. But you still have to move. You still must trust that the steps you're taking are shaping your path, even if they're small. It's about having the faith to keep walking even when you can't see the destination. Confidence. Direction. Patience. And how sometimes, you won't know exactly where you're going, but you've got to believe you're being led. That somehow, moment by moment, it's all coming together.

Let me pause right here and offer a prayer from my Bible app that stuck with me:

"God, I need You. You have given me everything I need to live a godly life. But that doesn't mean it's easy. Please help me to not waver in my faith. Help me to be on guard against any attacks or lies from the devil. Give me the courage to live for You every day. In Jesus' name, Amen."

Here's a quote I read the other day that really stood out:

"I alone cannot change the world. But I can cast a stone across the waters to create many ripples." – [*Mother Teresa*]

That's powerful. And here's another:

"You've become so damaged that when someone wants to give you what you deserve, you don't even know how to respond." [Courtney Peppernell, *Pillow Thoughts*]

Sometimes we have been so hurt that goodness feels foreign. But let me tell you: Your refusal to stay in a life you don't want must become stronger than your fear of the unknown. God has more for you. Your best days are not behind you. There are still mountains to climb, battles to win, dreams to fulfill.

I truly believe this: when you tap into the power of God, you begin to step into your full potential. You become more of who He created you to be. He chose you. He gave you gifts, He gave you a role, and if you haven't figured out what that purpose is yet, ask Him.

That's why I'm writing this book.
That's why I'm building a business.
That's why I'm praying for the love of my life.
That's why I want children and a family.

He wants us to create.

God knows my heart. He's the Waymaker. He's the Promise Keeper. And I trust that He's going to bring all of this together, in His time. Maybe tomorrow. Maybe a year from now. But I keep walking. I keep praying. I keep expecting.

Because I believe He made me to be a husband, a father, a leader, a writer, a disciple and a son.

And as I walk through mountains and valleys, I grow. I become more patient. I gain more endurance. I move from man to a patriarch. And it's not always easy. But it's always worth it. Remember: Love God. Love, your neighbor. Repent. Pray without ceasing. Invite the Holy Spirit to capture your thoughts. Be vulnerable. Take risks, even with your heart. Guard it, yes, but don't be afraid to step out in faith.

I want to be a Gideon.
I want to be a David.
I want to be a Joshua.
I want to be a Daniel.

I was reminded today that God brings people into your life for a reason. And you only see those reasons when you're paying attention.

So today, I thank God. For my life. For my home. For my Chihuahua, who turned 11 today. (Happy birthday, Calvin.) I thank Him for my family and friends. I thank Him for the breath in my lungs. For Jesus. For His sacrifice. In Jesus' name, Amen.

Let me close this chapter with one more thought: We reflect on the things at the end of our day. Sometimes we're physically tired. Sometimes mentally. And sometimes both. But in those quiet moments, we think about what we did right. What could we do better? And we try to learn from it.

There are so many variables we can't control. So many outcomes that change based on the smallest things. But if you did everything you could, if you truly gave it your best, then let the rest go. Because the things outside your control, those belong to God. That is, if you will give it all to Him.

One last thing about confidence: I heard someone say that "confidence is just isolation of comparing yourself to others." But true confidence, Godly confidence, isn't about comparison. It's about knowing who you are in Him. Trusting that your identity is secure.

Because the world will tell you to compare, to envy, and to judge others. To tear others down just to feel better about yourself. But that's not who we are called to be. When someone cuts you off in traffic or drives too slowly, you may want to lash out. But pause and ask: why am I comparing myself to this person? Why do I think I'm more important? Where's my grace? Maybe the person in front of you is elderly. Maybe they have a disability. Maybe they're on their way to visit a loved one in the hospital. You just don't know.

So instead of comparing yourself, pray for them. That's the real test of confidence. Not in what you say about yourself, but how you treat others.

You want to be confident? Stop comparing. Start loving. Start walking in your calling.

AT THE END OF THE DAY

There's something about the end of a long day. You walk in
the door, drop your keys on the counter, and exhale.
Sometimes, that exhale carries the weight of everything
you thought today would be but wasn't. You start replaying
moments in your mind, comparing what happened to what
should've happened. But that's the thing, we don't get to
know how our days will unfold. We don't get a heads-up
about the emotional rollercoaster we're about to ride.

And honestly? That uncertainty frustrates a lot of people.
Today was one of those days for me. The kind that ends
with a knot in your chest and a head full of "what ifs." But
the difference is, if this had been a few weeks ago, my
attitude would've been a lot worse. I know that. I *feel* that.
Something's growing in me. It's not a full revelation yet,
but it's different. I'm different. And I thank God for that.

There's still a part of me that hopes this person comes back
so I can help them, so I can finish what I started. But
driving home, I found myself slipping into old thoughts.

Telling myself it was just another boring day. Telling myself I'm broke, even though I'm not. Telling myself I'm stuck in a loop. That I'm heading home to do the same thing. Go to bed, get up, and do it all over again.

And you know what? We've all been there. That's the human condition. That's where God shows up, in the middle of our weakness. When we're drained, when we're tired, when we're feeling underpaid and undervalued. That's where He comes in and reminds us: *You were never meant to carry all of this on your own.*

We think we're better than we are sometimes. We set unrealistic expectations and then beat ourselves up when we don't meet them. I want to succeed. I want to do big things and earn my living, not for ego, but because I want to build a future. Write this book. Start a family. I want to pour my love into them and build a legacy that matters. God knows this. My Father in Heaven knows. And I believe He's preparing me. That this process, this season, is part of that preparation. I'm not there yet, but I'm not where I used to be either. That's growth.

At the end of the night, when we finally sit still, it's easy to let discouragement creep in. And yes, the enemy waits for those moments, when we're tired, when we're weak, and when we're questioning. But what I've learned is that humility is stronger than discouragement. When I come home with an open heart and lay it all down at God's feet, He meets me there. He fills the gaps where I feel empty. He reminds me that I don't have to figure it all out. That's not my job.

And can I be real with you? I've heard something that stuck with me, "Don't be arrogant in your confidence. Don't be so sure of yourself that you leave no room for God to move. Because true confidence doesn't come from pretending you've got it all together. It comes from knowing who holds your future. That kind of confidence is secure. It's rooted. And it doesn't come from comparison. Comparison kills confidence." [*Pastor Steven Firtuck*]

You can't look at someone else's highlight reel and measure your worth with it. You can't walk into Walmart or a five-star restaurant and start sizing yourself up against everyone else. Because someone is always going to have more, look better, drive a fancier car, and own a giant house. And someone else is going to have less. But that's not the mission. The goal is to be confident in *who God made you to be*, not the person your mind projects yourself to be.

Even Scripture tells us: don't compare, don't judge. Don't assume you know someone by how they look, talk, or walk. You don't know their story. And no one knows yours unless you share it.

That's why I write. That's why this book exists. I'm not perfect. I don't have it all figured out. But I *do* have experiences. I've got 45 years of life under my belt, some good, some broken, some victorious, and some still in progress. I want to use all of that to encourage you, to point you to the Bible, to say, *hey, I've been there. I get it. Let us walk through this together.*

You do not have to take my advice. You can read this and toss it aside. But my hope is that something I share, some story, some scripture, some struggle, maybe it'll connect with something in you. Maybe it'll open your eyes to God's love in a new way. That's my prayer. Because at the end of the day, I want to come home holding my head high; not arrogant, not proud, but confident that I did what I could. That I loved people well. That I served with integrity. That I listened more than I spoke. And that I left the results in God's hands. Confidence isn't loud. Sometimes, it's just the quiet peace of knowing you're walking the right path, even if it's hard. Even if no one claps for you. Even if the paycheck doesn't match the effort.

I'm working on projects around the house that are difficult, challenging, and give me a heightened sense of learning and accomplishment. Remodeling isn't my comfort zone, but I'm learning. I'm growing. Because transformation always looks messy in the middle. And I know when it's finished, it'll be worth it. Same with this book. Same with my calling. Same with my life.

God's timing is better than mine. His provision is greater than my effort. His vision is bigger than my dreams. So, I'll keep writing, praying, showing up, and trusting. I'll keep believing that my wife and children are coming. That the business will grow. That the purpose He planted in me will bloom in season. And tonight? I'm signing off to go pray. Not because I'm discouraged, but because I'm grateful. Because I know He holds tomorrow.

And that's all the confidence I need.

LEARNING THROUGH THE FIRE

It's not just about what happens to you in life, it's about how you react *afterwards.* How you process it, or what picture you paint with the pieces at your disposal. That's where perspective comes in. You may not be able to control every outcome, but you *can* control your response. You *can* decide how to handle it, how to learn from it, how to grow *through* it.

And let me tell you: growing through something doesn't mean you get the answers right away. It's hard. One of the hardest things you'll ever go through, if you're doing it right. But if you lean in, if you stay in the fight and let God shape you, it will change you. Deeply. Slowly. Permanently.

This isn't instant. It's slow, refining like gold in a fire.

But if you live in the *moment,* like God tells us to, if you stop panicking about your future and simply *live,* you'll start to feel the difference. Plan. Dream. Set goals. But don't *live* in the future. Don't get so focused on what *could be* that you miss what *is.*

Because if all you ever do is chase the future in your head, you'll never enjoy what's right in front of you. That dream will become a myth. A mist. A blur. Like you imagined it but never lived it. See, a lot of people dream of escaping their current life. But God's asking you to slow down and *live* it. Don't rush through it. I can promise you there's no short cut to life. Resist piling every bucket list item into a single week or a crazy month. Live life to the fullest, *but one day at a time.* That's what He means.

You *should* dream big. Believe in love, chase your calling, and build a life that brings you joy. But it takes time. And while you don't have *infinite* time, you *do* have *this* moment. So, why not live in it? Discipline and focus are how those dreams become reality. That's how you go from storm to breakthrough. That's how you *live now* so you can live your dream *later.* Because if you're willing to *work* through the storm, I promise you'll *walk* through the dream. The Lord promises that, too.

It's your faith. It's your belief in Him. It's your refusal to quit. Just keep moving. Just keep swimming. Just keep believing. I've had a couple of powerful nights with my men's group lately, enduring deep discussions over Galatians, Hebrews, and Romans. It's amazing how the Bible ties itself together. One verse links to another, then another, until you see the full picture. And it's true. [David Paul Kirkpatrick] *"We don't read the Bible; the Bible reads us."* It knows what you're dealing with. It's *alive.* It's real. For the kids, the teens, the grown adults, you are reading this right now. I promise you; God's Word is alive and real. He *will* guide your steps. He *will* bless your journey. But you must abide in the truth. You must believe that what He says is true because He's faithful.

If you don't believe that, you'll miss the very thing God's trying to give you. It's not that He disappears. *Know* Him. *Seek* Him. Lean not on your own understanding, but in *all* your ways, acknowledge Him, and He will direct your path.

One of the Scriptures I hold close to my heart—one I read every night after my men's group—is Hebrews 10:23:

"Let us hold fast to the confession of our hope without wavering, for He who promised is faithful."

That Scripture has transformed me. Something blossomed inside of me. It's shown me that my hope and God's promise go hand in hand. That it's okay to be alone for a time. That you must learn to love yourself—not in pride, not in arrogance, not in ego—but in reverence.

So, follow Him. With every breath. With every step. Even when you can't see the whole road. Put on the full armor of God. That armor is your protection. And notice, there's nothing for your back. Why? Because God's got it. He's behind you. Jesus is leading you. The Holy Spirit is inside you. You've got the Holy Trinity surrounding you. You have everything you need. Even in a dark world, you can see clearly, because *He is the light.* And that light is in you. So, breathe. Move. Trust. And know that even if the path isn't fully lit, Jesus is still your lamp. He's your guide. You don't need to know *everything.* Just take the next step. Just do *your* part. You are not alone. And this is not for nothing.

I wouldn't be here writing this book without God. I wouldn't have even survived what I've been through without Him. You may never fully understand the depths of pain everyone experiences. The nights crying until there were no more tears that would drop. The despair. The confusion. The rock-bottom moments you thought you wouldn't crawl out of. But you *do* understand. You've been there too. Or you're there *right now.*

You don't always see the storm someone else is going through. You don't know what they're carrying behind the smile. That's why we need to *stop being hateful.* And too many people are pretending they're okay when deep down they're falling apart. This world teaches us to fake it. To hide our truth. But healing only happens when you get *real.* Real with yourself. Real with God.

Sometimes people come off arrogant or critical, not because they're evil, but because they're broken. Their criticism is a mask. Their judgment is protection. That's why it's so easy to give advice from the outside. So easy to point fingers at someone else's relationship or parenting or life choices without ever addressing your own mess. And yes, I've been guilty of that too.

I'm learning that sometimes I overwhelm people trying to help them. I see potential of what *could* be. But I'm learning that not everyone is ready for the whole picture in one sitting. People change when *they* decide to change. When they're ready, they *want* it. I can't change you. Only *you* can do that. But I can speak truth. I can share my testimony. I can remind you; you *can* grow. You *can* become who God made you to be. But you've got to want it. You've got to let go of the crutches you've built your identity on. They're holding you back. Just because your life looks stable doesn't mean it's rooted in truth. Let God show you what needs to shift. Let Him strip away what is fake and fill it with what is *real.* Because I promise you, when you let go of the illusion, *that's* when transformation begins.

So, if you're still here reading this, then I believe this is for you. Let go of the fear. Let go of the pressure. Let go of the act. And let God in. You're not too far gone. You're not too broken. And you're not alone.

God has your back. Jesus is lighting your path. The Holy Spirit is moving within you. Keep walking.

FAITH REQUIRES ACTION

I know how this may sound, but at the ripe and tender age I'm at right now, I know I can make a difference. I know I matter. I know I have something to say, not just because of where I've been, but because of where I'm going.

I'm someone who has chosen to keep a clean mind. To take steps forward in the direction of God's path, not my own. I know that I've got the Father behind me, the Holy Spirit inside of me, and Jesus leading the way in front of me. I've given Him my heart. I've bowed my knee. I've given Him my truth. Which means I've given Him my love.

He has me, **because** I've surrendered.

And with that surrender, He has my faith. Because He *is* my faith. And I follow the Lord. I follow my Savior and the Holy Spirit. He is the one who speaks to me. He directs my steps. Sure, I may have my own ideas. I may put things into motion and make plans in my head. But I also know those desires are planted by Him. I speak them out, I pray over them, I give them back to Him. Because when I speak them in truth, when I speak them in faith, something begins to move.

I saw something the other day that blew my mind. It started with the word *distraction*. Take the "dis" off—and what do you have? *Traction*. Take the "tr" off that—and now you've got *action*. – [Nir Eyal – *Indistractable]*

See, you must get rid of distractions before you gain traction. And you need traction before you gain clarity. But nothing happens without action. If you don't move, you won't see what God is trying to do next. You won't see the result of obedience unless you obey.

There's cause and effect. There's action and reaction. There's faith and there's fear. There's discouragement and there's hope. And you get to choose which one you follow.

Lately, I've been reading 1 Samuel and 2 Samuel, and I've fallen in love with the story of David and Saul. It's powerful. It's humbling. There's this overwhelming sense that God is so intentional. That His hand is on it all, even when it's messy. Even when people betray. Even when people are afraid.

It's been a major transition for me. This word, this season, it's deep. It's new. It's beautiful. And I love it.

I'm literally praying as I write this because God has been *so* good to me. My Savior has carried me. These fears and weaknesses I keep talking about in this book. They're not just theories. They're mine. They're real. And I'm speaking to you from experience.

I'm sitting in my kitchen, headphones on, blocking out the world, speaking into a mic, letting the Holy Spirit flow. This isn't prewritten. It's not polished. This is coming raw, real, and straight from my spirit. And one day—maybe you're reading this right now, it will all be part of a book. I hope it changes lives. Because it's not just from me. It's from God, through me, to you.

I'm not here to tell you how to live your life. I'm here to tell you that there's truth—and that truth is found in Him. If you go to the Word on your own, if you seek Him genuinely, you *will* find Him. You don't need anyone else to tell you who you are. You just need God to reveal it.

And don't tell me you're alone. Because if you have Him, you're never alone. But how deep is your family rooted in God? How deep is your relationship rooted in the Word? What kind of spiritual legacy are you building for your children, your home, your circle?

Maybe your family is already full of faith—and that's amazing. But let me ask you this: who are you helping with that blessing? Who are you discipling? Who are you leading to Christ?

Because if you've been raised in the Word, if you've been walking with Him for years, then you *should* be leading others. You should be planting seeds. You should be telling people about Jesus. Not forcing it. Just sharing it.

Because it's not about converting people by pressure. It's about loving people through truth. Let them come when they're ready. Let them seek Him the way you did. The way I did. The way we all have to.

My truth may not be your truth. But *God's* truth is for all of us. And it will tell you exactly who He is.

YOU ARE NOT ALONE

You don't walk this life alone. Not for a second. Every step you take, God is already there. Jesus is leading the way, the Spirit is guiding you from the inside, and the Father is behind you, steady and unshakable. You are surrounded, upheld, covered. That's the reality you can hold onto. It is easy to forget, though. We live in a world full of noise and distraction. We see people rushing, striving, and trying to control everything around them. And in the middle of it, it's easy to forget that God's timing isn't ours. He doesn't rush, He doesn't panic, and He doesn't miss a step.

I have seen it in my own lifetime, when I thought I had it all figured out, only to realize that what felt like a setback was protection. Doors I thought were closed too early, delays I thought were frustrating, even mistakes I wished I could erase were all shaping the path I didn't know I needed to walk. God's redirection often comes disguised as inconvenience. This is where attention matters. Not distracted attention, scrolling through life, or checking boxes. I mean intentional awareness. Watch how people speak to you, how your words come out in response, and how your heart reacts. Pay attention to your routines, your small decisions, your habits. Are they aligned with who God is calling you to be? Are they building life, or draining it?

Kindness is part of this awareness. You never know what someone is carrying behind the smile they wear. People lash out because they're hurting, because life has beaten them down in ways you can't see. That's why forgiveness, patience, and compassion aren't just virtues—they're lifelines. Love heals. It transforms. And transformation isn't about forcing change on someone else. That only breeds resistance. True change begins inside, with surrender and willingness. You have to decide that you want to grow. You want God's guidance in every choice. You want to be shaped by His truth, not by my comfort or pride.

Obedience in the ordinary matters. Show up. Do the small tasks. Serve quietly. These actions, repeated faithfully, create a foundation stronger than any sudden success. For me, that looked like working traffic control at my church— a simple act, but one that taught me humility, patience, and consistency. Your gifts, used faithfully in small ways, connect to God's purpose in ways you can't always see immediately.

Prayer isn't just asking, it's aligning your heart. Scripture isn't just reading, it's calibration. Discipline isn't a burden, it's freedom. Every tear you've cried, every question you've whispered, and every dream you've held close— God knows them. He is moving, even when it feels invisible.

And when doubt whispers— "Why now? Why them? Why not me?"—remember this: patience is part of the walk. Forgiveness is part of the path. Redirection is part of His care. You don't have to see the entire story to trust the Author.

So, walk steadily. Speak carefully. Listen intentionally. Choose joy. Choose love. Choose obedience every day. Step by step, day by day. God has your back. Jesus leads the way. The Spirit is within you. And when you live with that reality as your guide, peace is no longer a concept—it's your companion.

Live it. Walk it. Show up. You get to.

THE BATTLE AFTER THE BREAKTHROUGH

After you've gone to church, read your Scriptures, and given your time to God in the morning, you feel this incredible surge of motivation. You feel inspired to go out and do the things that will make your life line up with your purpose. Then the enemy comes. Right after you've been lifted, energized, and ready to push toward your destiny. There's this middle-of-the-day slump of complacency that creeps in.

Maybe you were fired up to write, work on your dreams, start that business, or even just to read your Bible. But suddenly, your mind is whispering: "You've done enough. Take a break. Go relax. Forget the discipline." And you might start rationalizing maybe I should just scroll endlessly on my phone, play a video game, or get lost in some distraction. The enemy is working to rob you of the momentum God gave you.

Discipline, consistency, and patience are what separate those who achieve from those who plateau. Motivation is temporary. Inspiration is fleeting. Discipline is permanent. And it carries you through the moments when your energy fades, and Satan deceives your heart and mind.

Even Paul talks about it in Romans; our sin, mistakes, and tendency to conform to the easy way out. I've known what it's like to follow the crowd, let culture and the opinions of others define me. And it never works. The road less traveled is where Jesus is and where transformation begins. But it is uncomfortable and scary. It makes you confront your weaknesses and your fears. Jesus is asking you to start somewhere you don't want to.

Let's be honest, life will always throw distractions at you. Friends, family, social obligations, and emergencies. You get all fired up, the day slips by, and suddenly your momentum is gone. That's why you must build consistency into your life. You can't rely on fleeting inspiration. You must project your goals, write them down, plan the steps, and stay disciplined, even when it's inconvenient. Even when the world screams, "Just quit, relax, and conform."

Life will hand you losses and disappointments, sports teams lose, projects fail, people let you down. But here's the point: these things do not define you. You are not the sum of circumstances out of your control. You are the sum of your choices, your discipline, and your obedience to God. Stop letting the world dictate your mood, your confidence, or your sense of purpose. This is about perspective.

Conformity is easy. The crowd takes the easy road. Jesus walks the long way. Remember when Jesus took the disciples to see the Samaritan woman at the well? This was the long road to where they were initially going. All because He needed to transform her. He takes you into the uncomfortable and unfamiliar. A place where your fears meet His power. You push through and do the hard work. Fight for patience, understanding, and obedience. Consistence builds your life into something that lasts.

And yes, there are temptations; social media, instant gratification, distractions that promise quick results but steal your soul. They are everywhere, and they will try to derail you. But you get to choose. Your eyes, ears, mouth, and mind are doorways. You choose what comes in. You filter it. You discern it. You guard yourself from what doesn't build you up and doesn't align with your purpose. Draw closer to God.

Isolate yourself from the distractions. Dive into His Word. Let the Holy Spirit guide you. Listen to that still, small voice inside. That's God's truth. But you won't hear it if your life is cluttered with noise, nor will there be any action if you're following the crowd. Discipline yourself, guard your heart, your mind, and stay faithful to what God has called you to do.

You may stumble and fail. That's okay. You will make mistakes. Keep moving forward, even when it's uncomfortable and when no one else understands why you're doing it. When you stay on that road less traveled and follow the path Jesus sets before you is where real life begins. Your purpose, joy, and fulfillment are found only in Him.

I've been watching *The Chosen* lately, finally getting through the entire series, even though I missed a few episodes here and there. And now, it's constantly playing through my house. At the same time, we have started a full construction project in my hallway. My living room carpet and the laminate wood in the kitchen were removed. Transformation is happening, not just in my home, but in me, too.

And this brings me to what I want to share with you, the readers. Nothing in this world can truly block what God has for you. Obstacles are often created in your own mind. I'm not perfect, and neither is anyone else you look up to. We all fall short. But if you take a step back and see it, your life, your circumstances, they're all lessons which shape you.

So how do you align yourself to receive what God wants for you? You must be in the right mindset. You can't just read my words and expect them to hit; you must bring yourself to Him. Your connection with Jesus, patience, and willingness to gro. This makes the difference. Answers don't come all at once and life isn't designed to be comfortable; God's truth is patience, and it's sometimes challenging.

Think about Judas. He followed Jesus and believed His teachings, but he became impatient, which led to betrayal. And yet, everything that happened was part of God's plan. Impatience can derail you and make you step off the path. But when you let Jesus lead and trust Him to guide you through life, you will find peace.

And yes, that includes relationships. Whether you're a man or a woman, God comes first. Your role as a spouse, a parent, a leader, these are sacred. They exist within the framework of God's guidance. Allow Him to define your path and the rest falls into place.

Life's complexities often come from our insistence on controlling things. We want comfort and demand instant results. God's way is slow, deliberate, and intentional. He wants you to mature and understand His timing is perfect. It will feel uncomfortable at times, but it's a necessary kind of hard, the kind that builds your character.

Here's what I want you to hold on to: God's love is real. His guidance is true. And His plan for your life is good, full of hope and purpose. You may not understand it now, you may be impatient, you may be questioning life but trust Him. Follow His path and listen to His Spirit. Let Him mold and prepare you for the life He has intended for you. Love Him first with all your heart and love others as you love yourself. Serve and care in ways that reflect His love. This is the path to joy and fulfillment through Christ. Let God lead and be steadfast. Walk boldly in His truth because the life you've been seeking is not a distant dream.

What matters is that life keeps moving, and I keep learning, growing, and trusting God in the process. There's a difference between following Him and living what you follow. If you're truly following, you are living. But living doesn't make you flawless. What I want to stress is patience, humility, and vigilance. Life is full of challenges that stretch us to the brink of exhaustion. When we encounter them, we can either run or grow. God doesn't promise a life without trials. What He promises is His presence in every difficulty and walks with us, when we're falling short. Stop using God as a fire extinguisher and only call on Him when things go wrong. Praise Him on your good and your bad days. Ask for guidance but always remember to thank Him and reciprocate love.

Impatience will throw you off the path. Judas had faith; however, he lacked patience, and we know how that turned out. When we trust God, we walk the path set before us and must wait on His timing. He doesn't rush; He teaches, He grows, and He strengthens us as we go. Self-control, humility, patience, kindness, these are not just things we practice with others. They start within us, in how we treat ourselves and how we treat God. When you control your reactions, you're exercising your faith as much as your discipline.

Your greatest growth comes through the hardest challenges. You don't need to pray for life to be easy, but for life to be transformative. Instead, pray for problems which challenge you, because that's where God's grace becomes visible. Going through trials with God by your side is far more rewarding than being carried around the storm. Praise Him when you're feeling defeated. Thank Him for the breath in your lungs, lessons in your pain, and for His constant presence. The enemy attacks hardest when you're closest to your purpose. But God is greater than the struggles and He's already given you the tools to rise above. Make every effort to trust Him and keep taking steps forward. Allow the grace of God to be noticed and rewarded. It's available to everyone who seeks it, even in the darkest valleys. Weaknesses and fears will come and go, but God's love is unwavering. Let Him guide you through it all. In Jesus' name, Amen.

This morning, I was reminded of how God works through timing and opportunity. Moments like that remind me that our work has impact, sometimes long after we think it's done. I'm thankful that I can help take the next step into this new chapter of his life. I've been thinking about my own journey, and the life God has planned for me. I'm learning that time, which is freedom, is just as important. I have good work ethic, but the goal isn't to grind endlessly.

There is a bigger calling and a lot of it is sharing lessons from my life: lessons about fear, weakness, patience, self-control, and faith. To represent myself as a Christian Leader and accept I must speak and do. Listen to the word of truth and be a role model in Christ-like character. I've realized clarity comes through action. You can pray and plan all day, but at some point, you must move forward. God meets you in that motion. He doesn't ask for fifty-percent effort. He can take even one percent of your faith and multiply it beyond what you imagined. That's why it's so important to keep trusting Him, even when nothing seems to be happening.

I've been learning to take each day as it comes, even when it's hard. If you leave work or school frustrated and let negativity eat away at your spirit, it can lead to out of character reactions. If you pause and reset, you'll invite the Holy Spirit's strength in to replenish you. He will wake up your mind with a fresh perspective. Doing what you must do even when you don't want to, controlling your thoughts, your actions, your emotions. It's hard, but with God, it's possible. It's discipline.

Discipline comes in different forms. For some, it's doing chores they don't like or pushing through a stressful workweek. For me, it's writing this book while balancing my job, family, and responsibilities. Every step forward is part of my growth, and the challenge is shaping me for the next level.

Every day is a battle, "Take it one day at a time." One hour at a time, one moment at a time. It may sound boring, but it's how you stay grounded, how you maintain sanity, how you let the Holy Spirit guide your life. Life isn't perfect, but God's grace is. And if we stay humble, even through the mundane or frustrating parts of life, we grow and learn, which brings us closer to God.

I love what the Spirit's been pouring out because **now** feels like one of the most alive times yet. So let me give you a little picture of this moment. I'm sitting here with my headphones on, mic in front of me, and I've blocked out all my distractions. When I close my eyes and I let the Spirit flow. I can just speak and let God move through me. I'm writing the rough draft with all of you tonight. I'll go back and trim what needs trimming, then tighten things up. That's part of the process. I'm in love with where we're at right now, with the Holy Spirit in the room speaking through me.

And God opens doors in ways we often don't expect. I've seen it through men's groups, volunteering, and relationships. Doors open when you engage in faith and have the courage to take the next step forward. Abstain from fixating on one door. Sometimes we're staring at one opportunity, just waiting for it to open, while thousands of others are right in front of us.

I've experienced that personally. I want to be remarried and a family, but I know it must be the right person, at the right time, when we're both whole and ready. God doesn't give us people to complete us; we are already complete through Him. Relationships are in alignment with God's plan. We are all waiting for many doors to open. We have doors we're waiting to open that we believe will unlock our dreams and desires, career success, financial stability, or spiritual growth, etc.

However, we navigate those doors by prayer and trusting God is faithful, and His timing is perfect.

WHEN GOD MOVES QUIETLY

Some days, life doesn't follow the plan you thought you had. People don't act the way you hoped. Things break down. Opportunities pass by. And sometimes, it's easy to feel like the world is just a little too heavy.

But here's the truth: God is still moving. Even when you can't see it, even when it feels like nothing is working, He's working. And one of the ways He works best is through the small, overlooked details of your life.

Pay attention to the little things. The conversations you have, the gestures people make, the moments you usually rush past. They're not random. They're lessons, hints, or sometimes gentle warnings. That long red light that made you late dropping the kids off at school, maybe it kept you from an accident. That coffee you spilled just before leaving the house, maybe it delayed you from running into trouble. God often protects, redirects, and teaches in ways we don't notice until later.

And notice yourself. Your responses. Your feelings. Are you quick to complain, to judge, to lash out? Or are you choosing words and actions that bring life? You don't have to be perfect, but you do have to be aware. You can decide not to let your emotions dictate your actions. Feelings are temporary; truth is constant. I have had moments when I acted too quickly, skipped steps, or thought I could oversee something on my own. Every time, I learned the same thing: timing matters, guidance matters, and surrender matters. Sometimes the hardest part is simply stopping, asking God, and letting Him lead.

Life also teaches patience—not the abstract kind, but the practical kind. Waiting for an answer, waiting for people to change, waiting for circumstances to align. That's hard. But it's in that waiting that clarity comes. That's where perspective grows. That's where God shapes your heart. And here is another piece people forget: every blessing you receive, every opportunity, is also preparation. You can't give what you haven't learned to hold. You can't lead where you haven't been trained. That is why God shapes your character in the quiet, sometimes frustrating, everyday moments.

Be careful who you let influence you. Some people pull you backward out of fear or envy. Others move too fast and make you rush. Pay attention. Guard your heart. Let God guide who you listen to and what you act on. This isn't about stress or constant vigilance—it's about awareness. It is about living intentionally. Observing your own heart and the world around you. Choosing life in small, daily moments: what you say, how you respond, what you focus on. That's where faith isn't just a feeling, it's action.

Every misstep, every frustration, every moment of doubt can teach you something. And when you combine that awareness with prayer, with Scripture, with the guidance of the Holy Spirit, you start to notice the pattern: God is moving, even in the ordinary. Even in the mundane. Even in the "nothing happened today" days.

So, live like you're paying attention. Talk to God throughout your day. Listen. Watch. Take notes—not literally, unless you want—but mentally, spiritually. Let every interaction, every setback, every pause teach you something about patience, about timing, about trust.

The world pushes you to rush, to compare, to grab whatever you can. God asks you to slow down, to observe, to discern, to prepare. That's where peace lives. That's where clarity lives. That's where your life starts to reflect His. Every single day matters. Every choice matters. All the quiet unseen moments are shaping the person you are becoming. Notice them. Learn from them. Let God use them in you.

A WILLING VESSEL

There's something I found in the Bible not long ago that stuck with me, the word, *amanuensis*. It means a scribe, someone who writes a letter on behalf of another, often at their dictation. I'm writing what God gives me. I'm the vessel, the pen in His hand. It hit me even deeper as I've been studying Galatians, how Paul, possibly due to injuries sustained from being stoned in places like Lystra, may have dictated parts of his letters because his eyes or health were suffering. But despite the pain, the limitations, Paul kept pressing on. Whether his eyes were weak physically, or it was a metaphor for spiritual sight, the message stands: he did not let his weaknesses define him. He knew God's strength showed up when he could not carry on alone.

Paul wasn't perfect. I'm not perfect. You're not perfect. However, we are redeemed.

Just yesterday, I got upset with a co-worker. Not a big blow-up, but enough to rattle me. I am someone who communicates very well. So, when miscommunication happened, I let that sting get to me, and I showed a little bit of attitude. Five seconds of reaction. But it was enough. I knew it. And I had to own it.

Fast forward to today, my day off. Peaceful. Calm. I woke up early, set my mind right, decided to go grab a new pair of jeans, treat myself a bit. I jumped in my old car, just enjoying the morning. Then it happened. I ran out of gas on the side of the road, and the engine light was flashing. Now, the "old me" might have lost it right there and started complaining about how "the enemy was attacking me". However, I sat there in peace and opened my Bible app and started reading 2 Samuel. I prayed and waited. And you know what? God provided. A friend, who happened to take the day off two weeks prior, was able to help. What are the odds? God had that lined up in advance. I filled the tank. The car started. The engine light eventually turned off on its own. And I kept praising.

I'm telling you this story not just because it happened, but because God used it to redeem the attitude I showed yesterday. He taught me something. He juxtaposed the two days; yesterday's frustration with today's faith and showed me how I could grow in Him. Even my failure had a purpose.

That's what God does. He redeems our weaknesses, our broken places, and our fears. The very things that look like setbacks often become setups for learning, for deeper faith, for redirection.

And this ties right back into fear. Because fear tries to tell us to avoid discomfort. To walk away from hard conversations. To not trust again. But faith pushes us forward. Faith says, "You might've been hurt, but you're still here." You still have breath. And I'm not done with you."

I've had my heart broken worse than I ever thought I could survive. Some of you reading this know exactly what I'm talking about. Some of you are in it right now. You feel like there's no way you'll come back from this. But I promise you, you will. Not because of your strength, but because of His.

God will restore you. He will take the hurt, the silence, the lack of closure, and He will still use it for good. He's not interested in seeing you suffer forever. He's interested in refining you and drawing you closer to Him.

So yes, maybe your engine light is flashing right now, figuratively, or literally. Maybe your faith feels like it's running on fumes. But if you stop, breathe, and listen, you'll see that help is on the way. And maybe you'll realize that the help has already arrived, you just didn't recognize it at first.

That's it right there. He is faithful. Even when we are not, even when we doubt, and even when we fall short. Even when we throw a little attitude at someone who doesn't deserve it, He still shows up. And He still redeems.

You are not too far gone. You are not too broken. You are not alone.

So, keep going. Get back up. Let God redeem your yesterday through your today. And tomorrow, watch what He does.

God is fighting for you, even when you can't feel it.
Even when everything in you wants to quit. He's growing

you, pruning you.
He's trying to get you to grow up and walk in who He made you to be.

So, start living with faith.
Start loving with vulnerability.
Start moving with courage.
Start risking it all for the right things—because that's where your purpose lives.

And remember,
God first.
You second.
Love follows.
And a legacy is born.

FEAR NOT.

POSTSCRIPT

I really wanted to dive into this part because it is something that I produced on my own and I wanted to share it with you at the end of the book. I believe this can help every single one of you throughout your day when troubles begin to weigh you down. When you feel tempted and you are being taken through a difficult storm, just pray. Pray out to God and build that relationship with Him. Allow Him to work through you and truly leave your worries at His feet.

Pay attention at church when God is putting that sermon in your heart. Apply it to your life and open your mind for the upcoming week. You can transform your character to accept the wisdom that Christ gives you as guidance. Accept this truth and have the courage to start the week with a new perspective. Remember you don't need to wait for the next sermon to want that relationship with God. You can dive into His word at any time. You should always be immersing yourself in scripture. I understand all of us have a job and, daily errands and family. Additionally, some of us have activities outside of work and school during different seasons out of the year. I encourage you to set up a place in your home, your office, or reading room. Find your quiet place with God to block out every distraction and spend time in prayer.

Put your phone down and turn the television off. Get with Christ. You can take your Bible and a scripture for a full-on meditation with the Lord behind closed doors. You know Jesus died to save you from your sins, and He is your Redeemer. He is the one that paid the price for all of us, and God's grace leads us to accept salvation as a gift. He rose from the dead because of the power of God and the

Spirit that lives inside of us. He ascended to heaven and sent us the "The Advocate", who is in our hearts, souls, and minds.

Spend time with the Lord and mindfully know you are writing your life with Him. You are writing it together. He wants you to seek His Kingdom. In faith, picture the book of life and the pen in the room. You know you are in it because of the grace of Jesus Christ, because of the redeeming qualities that he has given us. Remember faith is seeing without believing.

Those days you're struggling, and you don't see Him, you will be tempted to pick up the pen and start writing on your own. Let God know all about your storm, drop everything at His feet and surrender. He will take everything. He knows everything that is going on in your life. Ask for the strength to hand over the pen and trust God.

We pray to Him when our storms are unbearable. We've all been there before. I'm not telling you you're wrong or ridiculing you for picking up the pen. I have done the same thing and started to write because it wasn't what I expected, and it wasn't right now. Countless times He has told me to put that pen down and that still small voice from the Holy Spirit has asked me, "What are you doing"? You're making decisions on your own, yet you know the consequences are written in ink. He gave you free will, and you don't see him because you don't feel like you're getting the response that you wanted.

You believe that you've prayed for something over and over again, but it hasn't happened. He wants you to talk to Him and discuss it. Go to Him with everything, always be talking to Him and always focus your gaze on Him. The rest of the world is out of your control, but God has everything **in** control.

Remember, if it doesn't come from God, then it's not his desire. If it's chaotic, it's not from Him. I assure you that if you believe what He promises is true, then you will choose the right way. You will lead a joyful and fulfilled life. You will be following in cadence with his footsteps.

Surrender the pen, with obedience and follow His next step.

ACKNOWLEDGEMENTS

First and foremost, I want to thank my Lord and Savior, Jesus Christ. Every word in this book, every lesson learned, every step of courage, comes from His guidance, grace and cadence. Without Him, none of this would be possible.

To my parents – Mom & Dad – thank you. Mom, your unwavering love, support, and patience have shaped me into the man I am today. Dad, though you may have passed in November, your wisdom, humor, and faith continue to guide me every day. It's an honor to be your son and walk in your footstep's sir. I pray that I can be the husband and father to my future wife and children, just as you were for me and mom. The creativity and freedom you allowed me as a child, the lessons you instilled about life and faith, have been the foundation for everything I pursue. I am so grateful to have been raised by both of you.

To my fiancé Alexandra - the woman I go into battle with every day. Your strength, love and unwavering support have carried me through this journey. You've motivated me in the completion of this book, but more importantly, you have strengthened me to face life fully, boldly, and faithfully. There is no one else I would choose to be by my side. I thank God for you and the girls in my life.

To my Aunt Carmen – your guidance and life advice have shaped me in ways that words can't fully express. Thank you for helping edit this book and for always being a part of my life and my journey. From the days of Blue Grass until now, you have been a constant presence and influence since I was a child, and I am deeply grateful.

To my best friend Dustin – your loyalty, encouragement, and belief in me mean more than words can express my brother. It's an honor to have walked through hell and back with you. *O'Captain, My Captain*

Ryan, thank you for your friendship, for the shared days of talking about our future wives and Law Enforcement and for continuing to carry that torch for the both of us with honor and dedication.

Jayson, my fellow sports enthusiast, and your brother Jeff – thank you for the countless years of friendship, shared victories, and life's ups and downs. The laughs, the lessons, and camaraderie we have shared have been invaluable.

To my cousin Shannon – your help, support, and guidance over the past few years have made an enormous difference. Thank you for always taking care of Calvin when needed.

Amy, thank you for your professionalism, creativity, and diligence for the cover art. Your work played a significant role in bringing the final product together, and I truly appreciate your contribution.

And to all my pastors and the men's group at Hope Lutheran Church in West Des Moines, thank you. Your guidance, encouragement, and prayer support have carried me through some of my most challenging days. Serving alongside you, especially in traffic control each Sunday, has been a blessing I will always treasure. I will keep shining my light at Corner 3!

Finally, to everyone who has touched my life in ways both big and small, who has encouraged me, inspired me, and walked alongside me – thank you. This book is as much yours as it is mine.

STEPS OF ENCOURAGEMENT

[Faith Baptist Church in Taylors, SC in February 2009. *"The Pursuit Of Manhood"]* You've got to heal your own soul before you try to heal someone else's. That's truth. That's discipline. That's love in action. You can't be pouring out of an empty cup and calling it noble. You're just draining yourself—and teaching your kids that self-neglect is love. That's not love. That's dysfunction.

So here's my model:

I go to God for provision; spiritually, emotionally, physically.
I steward my body, I work out and eat nutritious food.
I feed my spirit; I'm in the Word, I'm in church weekly, I serve, I disciple, I stay connected to other strong men of faith. I listen. I learn. I repent.
And when I fall short (and I do) I correct it. I redeem the moment. I don't let it slide. I pay attention, even to the bad stuff.

Because that's where God shows up. In the tension, trials, and the triggers.
He's saying, *"Stop retreating. Go forward."*

At the end of the day, I hope this whole book inspires you to look at your fears, your flaws, and your weaknesses, and stop running from them.

Attack them. Like Paul.
Own them. Like David.
Grow through them. Like Christ.

Stop complaining.
Stop playing the victim.
Stop going backwards.

Embrace the Daily Journey. Surrender, Faith, and Move Forward with God

Each new day is a precious gift from God — an opportunity to live fully in His purpose for your life. It's easy to feel distracted, discouraged, or stuck when things don't happen as quickly as we want. But God calls us to surrender control, trust His timing, and embrace the journey with faith.

Surrender Your Heart Each Morning
When you wake up, give God your heart and your trust. Tell Him, *"Lord, I surrender to You. I won't try to speed up the process or take the pen from Your hands."* Life can feel like a paradox going in circles and repeating the same struggles. But God's timing is perfect, even when it's different from ours. He's working everything out for your good.

Live with Expectation and Bold Faith
Don't just wish for change, expect it. Pray as if what you desire has already happened. This is faith: believing without seeing. Trust God's plan, even when the path is unclear. Release anxiety about rushing or slowing down. Instead, find peace in steady steps and an open heart.

Small Steps Lead to Great Blessings
God often blesses us through small opportunities. Handle the little things with care, and you'll be ready for greater things. Every morning, be thankful for your breath, your life, and the chance to grow closer to God.

Win the Morning Battle
Satan often attacks hardest in the morning, trying to discourage you and steal your progress. Don't let him win. Start each day with gratitude, prayer, and a willingness to listen for God's voice.

The Power of Prayer and Study
Prayer is powerful. Use it daily to seek strength and guidance. Dive into the Bible, join study groups, or explore devotionals that challenge you to grow. Don't be afraid to ask God for the big things — He wants you to dream boldly. But remember, greater blessings often come with challenges meant to shape and strengthen you.

Lessons from Gideon's Story
Gideon doubted himself. He came from a humble background and even hid in a winepress out of fear. Yet God called him a mighty warrior. When Gideon's army was whittled down from thousands to just 300 men, God showed him that victory comes through His power, not human strength. Like Gideon, you might feel small or unqualified, but God's strength in you is greater than any obstacle.

Take Steps in Faith, Even When You're Afraid
Accept God's calling and move forward, even when you feel vulnerable or scared. Each shaky step builds courage, and before long, you'll walk confidently in His purpose. You don't need a large army; God's power is enough to help you overcome every battle.

A Final Word of Encouragement
You have the strength to move mountains because God believes in you. Trust Him fully, take your steps forward,

and know that you are never alone. His power is with you every step of the way.

The End